Vendors
and Library Acquisitions

Forthcoming Topics in *The Acquisitions Librarian* series:

- Acquisition Plans, Jobbers, Vendors, and Book Dealers, Number 6
- Acquisitions and Resource Sharing, Number 7
- Gifts and Exchanges, Number 8
- Serials Acquisitions, Number 9
- Acquisitions and Collection Development Policies, Number 10
- The Collections Manager, and Training of Acquisitions Librarians, Number 11
- Acquisitions of Popular Culture Materials, Number 12

Note: The order of the series is subject to change

Vendors and Library Acquisitions

Edited by
Bill Katz

School of Information Science and Policy
State University of New York at Albany

The Haworth Press
New York • London

Vendors and Library Acquisitions has also been published as *The Acquisitions Librarian*, Number 5 1991.

The Haworth Press, Inc., 10 Alice Street, Binghamton, NY 13904-1580
EUROSPAN/Haworth, 3 Henrietta Street, London WC2E 8LU England

Library of Congress Cataloging-in-Publication Data

Vendors and library acquisitions / edited by Bill Katz.
    p. cm.
    "Also ... published as the Acquisitions librarian, number 5, 1991" – T.p. verso.
    ISBN 1-56024-121-7 (acid free paper)
    1. Acquisitions (Libraries) 2. Libraries and booksellers.
I. Katz, William A., 1924- .
Z689.V4 1991
025.2'33 – dc20   90-26656
                                                                                                      CIP

Vendors and Library Acquisitions

CONTENTS

ABOUT THE EDITOR

Bill Katz, editor of *The Acquisitions Librarian,* is internationally known as one of the leading specialists in reference work today. In addition to the two-volume *Introduction to Reference Work,* he is the author of *Magazines for Libraries* and *Reference and on-line Services: A Handbook.* Past editor of *RQ,* the journal of the Reference and Adult Services Division of the American Library Association, Bill Katz currently edits a magazine column in *Library Journal.* He is also the editor of the Haworth journal, *The Reference Librarian.*

Preface

Some 15 years ago Peter Gellatly and I tried our hand at a *Guide to Magazine and Serial Agents* (New York: R.R. Bowker, 1975). This is not a plug for an o.p. book, but rather a reminder that the analysis of the vendor/library relationship is hardly new. It is to this question that the authors of the present guide offer ideas and suggestions which should be of assistance to anyone working with serials and/or books and vendors.

From the first to the last expert in this manual an effort is made to establish: (1) The most efficient and satisfactory methods of selecting a vendor and/or jobber. (2) The way to gain expertise in evaluating the system. (3) The adroit and effectual ways to reach a successful relationship with the vendor and the public served by the library.

There is no one effective answer to the current goals. One may discriminate by careful selection of a vendor, or stretch the imagination by accepting and trying the various enhancements offered by this or that vendor. The truth, of course, is that there is no longer that much choice. As more than one contributor here points out, the real disadvantage today is the limited dynamics of a situation in which a half dozen large firms tend to dominate.

The present guide is in two sections, and begins with what probably bothers more librarians than any other aspect of the vendor relationship. This is the selection and the evaluation of said vendor. Approval plans, at least for larger libraries, are a major concern and these are dutifully considered by the experts in the last section. Well, not quite — one should point to the special report on the past, but far from forgotten editor of *Choice*. Anyone familiar with that journal will appreciate Mr. Bravard's study.

SELECTION AND EVALUATION— THE VENDOR SPEAKS . . .

One of the more outspoken, candid (and literate) of the vendors, Gary M. Shirk, suitably opens the discussion with a few challenges to librarians. What he terms an "awkward collaboration" summarizes the working partnership of librarian and vendor. To ease things a bit he calls for "openness, candor." The "unknown looms ahead," but this is one vendor with an appreciation of the future.

Representing Blackwell North America, R. Charles Wittenberg goes on to explain how the relationship of vendor and librarian has been drastically changed. The new technologies have made it both easier and more difficult, but not for failure of vendors to provide numerous new products. Many of these are explained here in detail.

Forrest Link explains how his Midwest Library Service offers a new collection development system. Books for College Libraries is the heart of the matter. Along the way Mr. Link does much to explain what a vendor can do, should do, and should not be expected to do. It's hardly a surprise that his words gear precisely with the preceding advice.

SELECTION AND EVALUATION –
THE LIBRARIAN SPEAKS . . .

The nightmare of the librarian is sounded in the second sentence of Brownson's acute analysis of vendor performance, e.g., "Some orders will never be filled . . . ." How this is to be avoided is explained by the Arizona State University librarian. He supplies all with a diagnostic tool "which is easily computed and facilitates vendor comparisons."

Twyla Mueller Racz and Trudie A. Root show how a medium sized academic library evaluates the pros and cons of the vendor, but, more important, give practical advice on budgeting and formula allocation and particularly the benefits of consolidation of orders with a single jobber. Frank Dowd "describes the process of developing bid specifications" and along the way the criteria for contract awards. It's hardly a smooth sail, but with a little planning the trip can be relatively smooth.

The Chicago Public Library as most large urban libraries serves numerous language groups. How does one obtain material for these readers? A foreign jobber often is the answer, at least where any volume is concerned. Fine, but as Linda S. Vertrees points out, there are complex problems – not to mention fun in the process.

This analysis will be of benefit to anyone who must go beyond the normal services of the American agent.

Richard P. Jasper moves in with the frequently expressed question, at least by vendors: "Do academic libraries expect too much of their firm order vendors?" It's more than a rhetorical query and the author explains how an honest reply will do much to expedite orders.

Getting down to specifics, and particularly the major headache of almost every acquisition librarian today, Jan Anderson offers "One step in containing serials prices." This is not merely moans and groans but positive suggestions on how to overcome at least some of the difficulties. Here the author is in harmony with previous contributors who suggest the benefits of consolidating orders.

The constant need to evaluate and re-evaluate vendors, services and particular library needs are sounded in all of these articles, and their practical application is evident. But another large, specific concern of equally large libraries is how to handle the ubiquitous approval plan.

APPROVAL PLANS AND VENDORS

Just what vendors, librarians and approval plans share in common is given in considerable detail by Mary J. Bostic.

She offers a convincing review of the literature in this controversial area and discusses the "transition from a traditional way of ordering books to approval order plans." This involves "matters of bibliographical responsibility and fiscal concerns." Her conclusion, as with others in this guide: "The ideology of approval plan program appears to be sound and shows the possibilities of bringing in a wide variety of useful materials."

Anna Perrault and Peggy Chalaron go a step further and discuss the details of an approval plan, or more specifically approval plans. In fact, the authors believe too little is written about multiple plans and they give detailed instructions on what to do and what not to do when setting up such an acquisitions program. Here it is interesting to contrast this view with the "consolidation" advice — although on different levels — of Racz, Root and Anderson.

The problem of the profile is considered by Sally Somers and in another piece by Gary J. Rossi. Both give practical, sound advice on the pitfalls of such profile approaches. The differences between what Somers calls a "closely defined approval plan" and needs of a smaller college library (Rossi) are instructive for anyone concerned with such important battle plans.

Lauren Lee describes a "number of generic and customized selection services" which vendors offer. Unlike previous contributors, the author moves into a discussion of nonbook and nonserial type materials which are currently of great interest to many libraries. Note, too, an extremely useful section which gets back to advice offered in the first part of this guide, e.g., "Questions for Vendors." Any librarian who puts these queries will save much time and effort.

SELECTION AND EVALUATION OF VENDORS – THE VENDOR SPEAKS . . .

The Wondrous Web: Reflections on Library Acquisitions and Vendor Relationships

Gary M. Shirk

SUMMARY. Libraries and vendors have long worked together in awkward collaboration. The benefits of that collaboration are demonstrable but may obscure a more fruitful working relationship. They should form strategic alliances to work toward long-term, mutually beneficial goals.

Those of us that have worked both as acquisitions librarians and vendors understand their relationship in a way few others can — viscerally. We have undergone the transmutation from librarian to vendor, and the creative tension of that relationship has become part

Gary M. Shirk is Vice President of Yankee Book Peddler, Maple Street, Contoocook, NH 03229 and formerly Head of Acquisitions, University of Minnesota, Minneapolis, MN.

1

of us. We have become comfortable with it. It is part of the pattern of the world we know. It is fact. It is right.

But you and I might wonder, if in our comfort, we forget something essential of the nature of things. Looking down the slope of time, we may confuse perspective with wisdom. The twisted path we have trudged merges with the background, the obstacles we noticed as we placed each step disappear, and the view simplifies as the jumbled terrain becomes softly rolling hills. We have become comfortable with the path we've taken. It makes sense to us just the way it is.

For fifteen years, I have witnessed libraries and book vendors contend with legal, ethical, and competitive pressures to build library collections. With determination and resolve, they have achieved an awkward "buddy system" and now shamble up that slope of time together. They stir up clouds of dust that obscure what is wrong with their collaboration and what should be done about it.

Maybe you and I have met before at the back of a crowded meeting room or outside in the hall between sessions on acquisitions or collection development. Maybe we spoke a few quiet words in greeting. Maybe we even took a few minutes to share fragments of our concerns.

If we had the time, if meetings hadn't called us away, and if we hadn't been afraid to open up and talk about what we don't fully understand, we might have sat down together and talked at length about library acquisitions and book vendors. We might have mused about the forces that bind them together and pull them apart. We might have questioned their traditional relationship and — perhaps — charted a new course, unshackled by the past and set free in the vast, unbounded future that lies ahead.

COLLABORATION

Few librarians today question the important role of the book jobber in their acquisitions strategies. In fact that role is gaining in importance as the book vendor assumes a more central supporting role in collection development, bibliographic control, and electronic data interchange. Book vendors have become as important to the continuing health of libraries as libraries are to the continuing well-being of vendors. The symbiosis is real and seems to work for both.

So, don't be surprised if you number yourself among the honorable ranks of acquisitions professionals or book vendors who see nothing wrong with the traditional collaboration. Perhaps you see the current methods of interaction as the result of constant and benign adaptation: libraries and vendors meeting every contingency, keeping pace with developing technologies, and – in short – evolving to meet present needs in the best possible way. You may point with pride to a system that advocates the use of multiple vendors, bids, periodic review and competition, confrontational negotiation, arms-length transactions, protective contracts, and reserved, disinterested communications.

The benefits to libraries, after all, are demonstrable. This system has evolved to protect the library from ethical controversy or to satisfy the legal requirements of the library's institutional environment. They have proven to give libraries higher discounts. They preserve the library's ability to negotiate and hold the vendor strictly accountable for service as stipulated in the contract. Open and continuous competition keeps the library up-to-date on all available services. The risk of a single vendor failure disrupting continuous acquisitions is avoided, and alternate vendors are always at hand.

Book vendors seem to thrive as well in this environment. They have fair and equitable access to most libraries. A large customer base is assured. Negotiations are up-front, candid, above-board. The contracts make expectations clear, delineate mutual responsibilities, and prevent misunderstandings. Vendors retain the freedom to develop and provide services as they see fit and sell these services to libraries in an open environment. They avoid being snared in the complex conflict-of-interest issues that plague public sector organizations.

Of course, you and I can agree to the benefits of our present approaches. We have often worked together to develop them. We would not have done so without seeing some mutual benefits. Nevertheless, as I peer into the dust our continuous shuffling has thrown into the air, I wonder if we have made the right choices, if better ways might exist, if under the cover of that dust the benefits we see in today's methods are less than what we might achieve. So, for a few moments, let's make a frank appraisal of some of the practices we have embraced.

The bid process, for example, warrants a closer look. If viewed from the perspective of the entire community of libraries, it has not achieved any of its primary purposes: higher discounts for libraries, equal opportunities for vendors, fairness to both parties, and freedom from ethical complications. Bids that achieve higher discounts for one library ultimately come at the expense of another. Lengthy, complex bids — often tailored to highly specific procedural needs — effectively shut out the small regional vendor. These vendors can neither afford the cost of filling out bid forms nor developing unique services.

For many libraries, the fear of uncontrolled award of the contract to low bidder is so great that the temptation to tailor bids to the skills of known vendors is nearly irresistible. For further protection, bids are filled with one-sided paragraphs that tie vendors tightly to terms (e.g., discount) while giving libraries escape hatches in case their commitments cannot be met (e.g., expenditure levels). Bids invite skepticism on the part of both parties and tempt both to unethical practices: the vendor to skirt discount commitments and the library to disregard promised expenditure levels. Nevertheless, vendors and libraries keep virtually all their promises and always have. Contracts have provided no additional guarantees.

In short, the bid system is costly, complicated, easily rigged, biased in favor of larger vendors — and unnecessary. Librarians already have less costly and rigid methods available to them. Existing techniques for periodic review of vendor services assure successful vendor selection in a competitive environment and provide for continuous performance measurement, evaluation of all elements of the relationship, and if necessary, change. Bids are clearly a case of well-intended actions gone bad.

Similar weaknesses appear in most other current relationships as well. Using multiple vendors, though assuring a larger customer base, burdens most vendors with many small accounts, increasing the average cost of every book shipped in this country. Confrontational or win/lose negotiation on discounts or other business conditions embeds an adversarial component in the relationship between the vendor and the library. Once again, what is lost to one library must be gained at the expense of another; or, if not, the vendor must reclaim the loss in reduced service to the contracting library itself.

Too much is made as well of the importance of arms-length transactions and reserved, disinterested communications. The complex and multifaceted collaboration between libraries and vendors cannot function well at arm's length. It must be direct, personal, unencumbered by professional posturing, and even passionate. The library and the vendor must know and understand each other well. The better this understanding, the better the library and the library user will be served.

Though clearly not bankrupt, the library/vendor collaboration is less than it should be. Perhaps now is the time for revolution, not more evolution.

STRATEGIC ALLIANCE

Where before you may have shaken hands with your vendor, now grasp both hands firmly and interlace your fingers. Join with a single book jobber or periodical agent in a strategic alliance, i.e., a long-term, mutually beneficial relationship aimed at achieving both library and vendor goals. Commit to working closely together, planning together, and celebrating success together.

To the library, this means locating a supplier/partner with whom you will work very closely to acquire library materials. It means accepting half the burden for communications. It means a willingness to change, to adapt your policies and procedures, to conform to standards. It means challenging tradition, debunking widely held "truths." It means constructive confrontation, clearly stated expectations, constant oversight. It means building confidence in your vendor through shared experience, knowledge, and planning. It means trust.

To the book vendor, the strategic alliance means seeking library partners whose objectives match your own. It means openness, candor. It means accepting the burden for half or more of communications. It means involving libraries early in your planning cycles. It means extraordinary efforts to achieve and maintain a secure, indepth relationship. It means sharing information, problems, solutions, and giving up — in part — control of your company to your customer.

It does NOT mean "Consolidation." Mark Twain inscribed on Pudd'nhead Wilson's calendar what was already a time-worn cliché, then added his twist to it: "Behold the fool saith, 'Put not all thine eggs in the one basket' — which is but a manner of saying, 'Scatter your money and your attention'; but the wise man saith, 'Put all your eggs in the one basket and — WATCH THAT BASKET.'"[1]

This is consolidation, a common practice becoming more common every day as valiant acquisitions librarians battle the dragons of inflation and differential pricing. But mere concentration of your orders with a single vendor, is not a strategic alliance for acquisitions. Let me add yet another twist to the cliché: "Put all your eggs in the one basket and GET IN THAT BASKET." Irrevocable commitment makes a difference to every aspect of the relationship and is the essence of the strategic alliance.

In exchange for this commitment, the library will achieve a stable source for books, services tightly integrated with its procedures, improved communications, better value, better quality control, and simplified order assignment. The library will minimize costly vendor selection procedures and performance monitoring will be simplified and focussed.

The vendor will achieve a stable, though perhaps more limited customer base. Order flow will become more predictable and more easily accommodated. Close customer participation in service design will assure positive reception to new services. The vendor will understand his customers' expectations more clearly and benefit from the integration of procedures. The alliance will reduce or eliminate the costly and problematic bid process.

The practical ramifications of the strategic alliance would be many and far-reaching. For example, the library might involve its vendor early in its automation planning. Its book vendor would be an integral part of the team selecting and installing a book acquisitions system. In similar fashion, the vendor might invite the library to assist with the development of its five-year business plan. Library staff would become privy to the vendor's competitive strategies and contribute their ideas to innovation in services.

Naturally, this degree of mutual involvement requires that both libraries and vendors overcome a plenitude of existing regulations and attitudes. For example, where bids are law, libraries would lobby for longer award periods with multiple extensions. Then work throughout the period to build the strategic alliance. Vendors, on the other hand, would have to embrace standards more fully, potentially giving up the "frills" that differentiate some of their services from their competitors'. Both would have to learn to share information fully with each other, but understand the need to keep some parts of this information confidential. The vendor, of course, continues to compete with other vendors and the loss of this information could damage the vendor's chances of success and weaken library/vendor relationship.

The strategic alliance blurs the lines between library acquisitions and vending. As the alliance strengthens, it becomes increasingly difficult to determine where acquisitions ends and vending begins. They move in harmony toward shared objectives, meeting challenges together. Their policies, procedures, and communications intertwine as they weave a wondrous web between them.

While recognizing its usefulness, we may fear as well as marvel at the web we weave. Many of us feel a chill run up our spine when we see a spider's web, but we understand that the spider's intricate construction is an engineering masterpiece: a trap, a home, a food storage system, an intercom. And, when the morning's light strikes the dew hanging from the web, we see it fully for the first time – at once potentially dangerous and beautiful.

CONCLUSION

Maybe we will fear the potential dangers of the web too much and never weave it. The unknown looms ahead. In a shadowed corner of our memory we may vaguely recall the opening stanza of the children's rhyme "The Spider and the Fly":

"Will you walk into my parlor?" said the spider to the fly:
" 'Tis the prettiest little parlor that ever you did spy.
The way into my parlor is up a winding stair,
And I have many curious things to show when you are there."[2]

The spider's intent is clear. So, we may fear the wondrous web because in the dark of ambiguity, the unmarked trail ahead, we wonder "Who is the spider? Who is the Fly?"

Maybe this fear is part of all change. We reach out to grasp what seems to lie immediately ahead but find no handhold. We wander toward it like a people in a dream, our objective floating ahead, obscure, wonderful and ominous. Each of us takes furtive, small steps — afraid to stride boldly. We stumble over unseen, frightening obstacles — creating hurdles even where none exist.

But perhaps when a history of the decade of the 1990's is written, it will describe how we overcame our fears, innovated, bucked the system, achieved success. I imagine a sober-faced, professional reception to the idea of strategic alliances, the denial of their necessity, the debate, the growing acceptance as pioneers achieve its benefits. I imagine a movement to strategic alliances beginning today and waxing as the decade matures. I see an airliner slowly overcoming its immense inertia and moving forward, gathering momentum, now away, free, at full speed, bursting through a curtain of apprehension and into the unlimited horizons of the new century.

REFERENCES

1. Mark Twain. Pudd'nhead Wilson. New York, New American Library, 1980. p. 113.

2. Mary Howitt, "The Spider and the Fly," in The Children's Book chosen by Horace E. Scudder, New York, Houghton Mifflin, 1909. pp. 146-147.

The Bookseller and the Dynamo

R. Charles Wittenberg

SUMMARY. The traditional library bookseller and his relationship to the libraries that are his customers has been dramatically changed by a decade of library automation. New products represent value added to the book in the box. Products and services are dictated by the needs of both collection development and technical services in the library. The results are as various as the systems and requirements of libraries.

You can see it in the photographs in the Blackwell companies' brochures. The long tradition of bookselling is suggested by images of the Bodleian Library's Gothic precincts and by the new world Gothic of the University of Washington's Graduate Reading Room. For generations scholarly libraries like these have filled their shelves with the help of middlemen who are experts at turning librarians' wishes into sturdy boxes of books.

The majority of photographs, however, are of Blackwell people at work at computer terminals or of endless rows of computer tapes. For us, as for our customers, the last decade has seen computer hardware fill our buildings and computer software occupy the foreground of our attention. The tradition of service — of responding to librarians' wishes — remains the core of our business. Those wishes, in the era of library automation, are more diverse, more complex, and more expensive than most of us had foreseen. We are pleased to be able to offer to our customers a steadily growing number of new products and services which change dramatically the way that they — and we — do our work.

R. Charles Wittenberg is Northeast Regional Representative for the booksellers B.H. Blackwell, Blackwell North America, and James Bennett.
Address correspondence to the author at P.O. Box 28, Hatfield, MA 01038.

9

TWO TECHNOLOGIES

Automation in the hundreds of libraries that we serve has moved ahead on two, largely separate, tracks: the implementation of large integrated systems and the amazingly diverse exploitation of the capabilities of PC's. The major turnkey system vendors all have something to offer to the acquisitions librarian and they have all thought — more or less — about the creation of interfaces between libraries and their vendors. For each new system that is chosen by a Blackwell customer there is an essentially fresh challenge to be met. The Blackwell automation people whose sole responsibility is developing and maintaining interfaces with our customers' systems, have become essential allies to the traditional bookseller. We want librarians to see us as eager partners in exacting the maximum benefit from their integrated systems and we hope that libraries will perceive our responsiveness in this sphere as a critical measure of our stature as a company.

The proliferation of PC's in libraries and the remarkable skills that librarians have developed in using them pose an entirely separate set of challenges. There are libraries for whom the PC based acquisitions products are an interim measure as integrated systems are chosen and funded and brought to maturity. There are libraries of smaller scale where PC solutions are sought or developed for the long term. And there are systematically automated libraries where PC functions supplement or interact with the integrated system, filling gaps and adding features. We respond as promptly and fully as we can to library requests for bibliographic or management data on floppy disks and we have seen a large network of customers grow up who send us electronic orders through our own "PC-Order" system.

"PC-Order" began as a relatively simple product through which libraries sent ISBN, Blackwell stock number, or author/title orders, and received in return acknowledgements and status reports for printing and filing, or for retention in the online file. As customers have sought additional features the product has grown to offer the ability to claim and cancel and to send queries about any bibliographic matter to Blackwell in North America and in England. It is widely used by major libraries to put foreign orders in the hands of a vendor on the day that they are created and at no postal or telecommunications cost to the library. Some customers use the interface of PC-Order with Bowker's CD-ROM Books in Print to create an online search and order capability. Electronic ordering is coming only slowly to the integrated systems and libraries of all types exploit their PC's for electronic speed of communication with their vendor.

TWO CONSTITUENCIES

The coming of automation to libraries, whether mainframe systems or PC products, has sharpened our awareness that as booksellers we serve two constituencies in the library. However the jobs are titled, and however the labor is actually divided, we serve both collection development and technical services. The traditional bookseller is a very different creature viewed by the collection manager, the selector, the maker and keeper of orders, and the receiver and payer of bills. Even in the smallest library where these functions are concentrated in one busy person, there are conflicting priorities and requirements, and the successful vendors are those who can add value to books in boxes by understanding how libraries really work and delivering appropriate products. Automation both complicates the matter and sweetens the solutions that libraries and vendors can create.

To date the automated environment has almost entirely focused our attention on benefits to be offered to technical services. Interfaces with roughly twenty-five commercial systems and a substantial handful of their homegrown counterparts take three book-related product forms.

The first is a "packing list" — a machine-readable bibliographic file sent to the library as a tape or disk or transmitted directly to the library's integrated system which also contains invoice information. The provision of a standard format bibliographic record together with price information looks to the simplest way that a vendor can move a cost from the library's books to our own: time (keystrokes) saved at the point that the boxes of books are received.

A second form of electronic record offers the library the ability to introduce a full LC MARC record into their system at the time a book is received. For our approval plan customers this may constitute an order, receive, pay, catalog and circulation record. These catalog records can be supplied with any book shipment of any order type and offer libraries both the immediate availability of a record and an enormous saving in the cost of catalog records.

The third automation benefit which the bookseller offers to library technical services is electronic ordering. Though not yet commonplace, the capability seems to have become a high priority for competitive system vendors. On the PC side electronic orders come both from our own system and through widely accessible e-mail networks. When orders can be processed directly into our mainframe, we share with the library the result of a quicker fill of the library's wants. As diverse as systems and PC applications are, we can meet the requirements of any book buyer dealing in MARC or fixed BISAC files — the almost common currencies of the realm.

NEW DIRECTIONS

The benefits the bookseller can offer to library technical services will doubtless both proliferate through the community and expand in number as new products and services are created by libraries and vendors working together. Just at this moment, however, we are strengthening the program of automation-related products that are directed to the collection development side of our customers' operations.

A "New Titles" (approval and standing order) bookfile numbering nearly 1,000,000 records, accumulated since 1970 in the U.S. and since 1979 in the U.K., is a unique Blackwell resource. It grows at the rate of 60,000 titles a year as new books are bought and "edited" into our New Titles systems. This data, created and stored in MARC format, has been supplied on an ongoing basis to libraries on paper forms that accompany their approval book shipments or, in lieu of books, through our New Titles Announcement Service. In addition we have offered Retrospective Collection Development services using the historical database. Given the scope of our New Titles program, this file approaches comprehensiveness in its coverage of the universe of academic publishing.

Together with our customers, and in response to their expressed wishes and needs, we are moving in several directions to integrate

New Titles services into the library's automated routines. Several integrated library systems offer (or allow) the capability to create an on-line book selection environment. Blackwell New Titles records can be tape or disk-loaded into customer systems and searched by selectors in the library – and outside where networks are in place. Public catalog search strategies offer quicker and more complex access points to new titles information than the paper records. Sharing records of desired titles between selector and order librarian is regularized, and systems create orders with a minimum of keystrokes on the technical services side. For years libraries have struggled to devise ways to circulate interdisciplinary and multi-interest title information to all interested parties, and this online selection tool responds to that need. Through the integrated catalog patrons, too, can be made aware of new titles available in the marketplace but not held or on order by the library.

Automated files have created new capabilities for retrospective collection development as well. We have been matching library holdings tapes against BCL3 in its machine-readable form and the results have proved to be a very useful analytical tool. Librarians have found, however, that the number of BCL3 titles in print is very low as half of the imprints in the model collection are earlier than 1970. To actually fill gaps in their collections many librarians choose the option of a holdings tape match with the Blackwell data base. The matching of holdings tapes against the Blackwell New Titles database is a product conceived by a customer and developed to provide lists for libraries of recent and readily available titles. Libraries select subjects, non-subject considerations and desired imprint range, and those "profiled" factors control the match. This response to one librarian's request has grown to be a very important and widely used service.

On the PC side we are prepared to deliver two additional products which link the selection and ordering functions. "PC-New Titles Announcement Service" delivers our on-going survey of the universe of publishing on floppy disks. Multiple search strategies embedded in the hard disk application give maximum access to new titles and since this selection tool may be linked to the PC-Order program, orders can be created and dispatched, if it suits the library's routines, entirely in PC mode.

"New Titles Online" responds to an often expressed desire on the part of our customers to use their PC's with a modem to query the Blackwell New Titles file. For collection developers using approval plans, this interactive dial-up system eliminates the uncertainty about book and profile matches by offering the capability to instruct us to "be sure to send on approval." For firm order customers a variety of search strategies provides access to roughly 80,000 recently published and soon to be available titles, with a built-in capability to create and send orders.

BOOKS

It was inevitable that the computerization of library operations would dramatically change the suppliers of that traditional paper and cloth centerpiece of the library's life. We are driven by customers' demands and we hope to be seen by them as partners in the business of acquisitions. For both the library and the bookseller the changes of the past decade have made heavy demands on talent and resources. Our electronic relationship with libraries has proven to be remarkably complex and far-reaching and expensive. We are committed to the future of this automated relationship—and to the traditional product as well: good books in sturdy boxes.

BCL3 (Books for College Libraries) and the Book Jobber: The Marketing of a New Collection Development Service

Forrest E. Link

SUMMARY. When the third edition of *Books for College Libraries* (BCL3) was released in 1988, it was available for the first time in a machine-readable format. At Midwest Library Service, the decision was made to obtain the tapes of BCL3 and investigate their possible application as a collection development tool which could be used to compare a library's holdings as reflected in their OCLC records to the idealized collection as reflected in BCL3. The hope was that this service would result in an increase of book orders for Midwest through both routine library expenditures as well as potential grants which this sort of project might engender. Several problems, some expected, some unexpected arose as this new service went into testing, but the early results suggest the viability of the project if potential clients are strictly qualified.

In the course of developing new programs, library service companies face several questions and decisions concerning feasibility, resource allocation, and marketing. This is the story of how Midwest Library Service dealt with the issues involved in launching a collection development project using the newly released, machine-readable version of *Books for College Libraries* (BCL3) as a data base from which customized bibliographies might be generated.

The scene is a conference room at the Bridgeton, Missouri headquarters of Midwest Library Service. It is the annual sales meeting

Forrest E. Link is the Northeastern Regional Manager, Midwest Library Service, 11443 St. Charles Rock Road, Bridgeton, MO 63044.

15

in 1988 and the discussion has turned to the new machine-readable BCL3. A bright and eager sales representative notes the imminent release of BCL3 and proposes that Midwest look into the possibility of producing customized subject bibliographies for customers. Another hits upon the idea of going a step further and comparing BCL3 records to OCLC records to identify gaps in library collections. As always seems to happen when sales people sense something new and exciting to sell, there is immediate assent and urgency. As also always seems to happen in such situations, the president of the company reacts with interest heavily tempered with caution. "Can we do it, and what will it cost?" Already, there are more questions than answers and the issue is set aside for investigation.

Answering the first real question about such an undertaking, "Will we be able to sell it?", seems easy. The sales department reports enthusiasm from the field for the idea. Pricing is an issue which will need to be addressed later as we assess costs and competitive pressures.

The practicality of this project is not so easily determined, and here there are two questions to answer. We need to get some idea of the actual content of BCL3 in terms of the potential availability from publishers of the titles it lists and we need to know the format of the tapes and how this will affect processing time and labor in producing lists of potential purchases.

From promotional literature, we learn that there are approximately 50,000 titles listed in BCL3 and that about 60% are new to the third edition. We also learn that nearly 98% of the titles in BCL3 are English-language. (Since Midwest is not an importer of books, this is considered good news, although there is no geographic breakdown of the number of US and non-US imprints.) But, because BCL3 contains no imprints later than 1987, we are concerned that the more time that passes before customer orders can be processed, the higher the out-of-print rate is likely to be and, consequently, the longer our project continues, the more likely it is that we will reach a point of diminishing returns where the costs of processing orders exceeds the profits from the actual books sold. This worry is tempered by our hope that some publishers will view the inclusion of their titles in BCL3 as a marketing opportunity too good to ignore and that they will bring back into print many of their listed titles, or that the reprint houses will pick up some of the slack.

REFORMAT TAPES NEEDED

The automation director calls the marketing manager for BCL3 with the next question and uncovers the first problem: BCL3 tapes are in ASCII format and Midwest's tape drives read only EBCDIC. This means that Midwest will need to reformat the BCL3 tapes and either ask for EBCDIC tapes from customers or reformat those as well. This translates to long processing times to make the tape comparison.

The costs are escalating and it looks now as though we will need to consider assessing some very justifiable service charge to libraries for running this tape match. This relieves the cost-conscious president, but dismays the sales force, who see the potential market shrinking as fees escalate. Now comes news that a competitor is offering a similar service at no charge. It's time for compromise.

If a BCL3 project at a given library can be shown to have the potential to generate a substantial number of orders which might not otherwise come to Midwest, the president will be willing to authorize a trial run without imposing any service charges. This will allow us to test the mechanics of the program and examine the publishers' fill rate without committing the company to a potentially losing proposition.

One of the sales representatives at Midwest has an extraordinarily keen nose for grant monies slated for library collection building. Shortly after the go-ahead is issued for the trial, he reports back with a prospective client. The amount of money involved is substantial and the library is very keen on the project. All we need to do is to compare the tapes and consider all non-matches as orders. They want to send us NOTIS tapes, not OCLC tapes, but because NOTIS is also in ASCII format our automation director is unfazed by this wrinkle, and the trial begins.

After a couple of false starts resulting from tape density incompatibility, we have the order list in a format which can be dumped directly into the computer. Out of approximately 20,000 orders, about 2,000 are immediately rejected as either foreign or order-direct presses. The rest are filled from inventory or ordered from the publishers.

As we begin to receive books and reports in response to this trial, a pattern begins to emerge. Our instructions to get everything we can that is not already in the library's holdings seem simple enough. What we have not counted on is the question of updated editions, title and publisher changes, and books in series. As a result, we are forced to begin doing an extraordinary amount of research on problem titles to avoid accidental duplicates. This brings about a resolve not to accept a project structured this way again.

From the field, another sales representative reports on another potential client who has grant funding for a large collection enhancement project. The customer is having her OCLC tapes readied for the installation of an integrated library system and can have them to us very quickly. She is, however, interested in only certain subject areas, not the entire BCL3 database. Is this a problem or an opportunity?

MODIFY THE SUBJECT PROFILE

The prospect of checking a library's holdings on a subject basis raises an interesting possibility. Conceptually, BCL3 may be viewed as any other bibliographic data base. In this case, we might use it as an approval data base. Since Midwest operates an LC-based approval plan, customers contemplating approval business with us commonly request an approval history printout which offers a detailed look at what titles would have been treated under specific profiling parameters. And since BCL3 provides LC class numbers in the tape, why not modify the subject profiling worksheet and treat the BCL3 comparison as we do an approval data base search? This would not only make it easier for libraries to examine their collections department-by-department, it would also potentially reduce our expense in the production of unused forms or unnecessarily long lists.

Another advantage of this approach became clear in light of the massive list of potential orders this first project generated. Approval books treated by Midwest are assigned a unique number. This number enables us to avoid keying into our computer complete order information for approval titles ordered as either added copies or in response to form selections. By taking advantage of the unique BCL3 number for each title and requiring it with orders placed in response to the holdings comparison, the labor of our order entry department is considerably reduced.

We now have BCL3 converted to EBCDIC and our automation director has had a program written which will easily (if not quickly) convert ASCII tapes. Although the results of the first trial are inconclusive, the sales manager prevails upon the president to permit another test under specific conditions: the customer must review the list of potential orders for the problems of duplicates, edition, and publisher changes and must agree to quote the BCL3 number in ordering.

The second test runs much more smoothly, although all are astounded by the size of the resultant list of potential purchases. This library has suffered from years of under-funding and is lacking over 30,000 of the BCL3 titles. The customer is relieved and grateful at the amount of manual checking the tape match has spared her staff, but at approximately $30 per title, this translates to a $900,000 need. Even assuming a 50% out-of-print rate, her grant will be woefully overspent. She decides to return only the most urgent portions of the list to Midwest for ordering and to fund as much as possible out of regular book monies over the next few years.

Although the costs and potential of the BCL3 matching program have not yet been fully determined, the major capital investments are in place. We have a workable procedure for handling the tapes and the order entry process is much streamlined by the use of BCL3 numbers. Still, there is more we can do to improve the operation.

The automation director, like many computer mavens, is an inveterate tinkerer, always looking for better ways to handle data. As we begin getting responses from publishers on the BCL3 orders, his staff begins to enhance the data base with information concerning availability so that out-of-print, foreign, or order-direct titles are intercepted before going into the system. It is costly for a vendor to repeatedly order material which will never arrive and it is inefficient for a library to fruitlessly encumber large amounts of money for a long period of time.

At this point, we still are uncertain about the rate of publisher response to BCL3 orders. Estimates now run at about 40% out-of-print. Under normal circumstances, this would be troubling to both Midwest and our prospective customers. But with the enhanced data base, titles previously determined to be unavailable are immediately reported to the customer and never actually ordered from the publishers. This eliminates the redundant and expensive handling of publisher reports on this fixed title list and helps to reduce the expense of the program. Handling new requests for BCL3 title matches should now be routine and our costs are predictable.

In the development of this new program there has been a natural tension between sales and management. The pressure of the former to move ahead with an exciting project has been tempered by the caution of the latter, anxious to enhance sales but always mindful of the costs involved. So far, the corporate consensus is that we are still not ready to offer the service unconditionally. We have decided against charging a service fee, but need to rigorously qualify potential clients. Our current expectation is that this service will remain available, but that as time goes on the interest in it will wane. There will be an increase in sales, but not as dramatic as hoped.

Perhaps the greatest value of the project will be in the enhancement in internal operations and automation and in the lessons learned in the marketing negotiations. The order-fulfillment staff at Midwest have expanded their repertoire of skills, the automation department has mastered new information-handling techniques, and the sales force has been stimulated to continue to think creatively with the support of management.

The customers have also benefitted from the new program. A few will take advantage of the BCL3 tape matching service, but the problem-solving skills and compromises which brought this project to fruition will be applied to many other as yet unforeseen operational or bibliographic needs.

Book Wholesaling:
Looking Toward the 21st Century

Larry Price

SUMMARY. The librarian relationship with book suppliers is a critical element in a library's overall ability to deliver quality service. Publishing and distribution has seen more change in the past ten years than in the previous one hundred. Librarians must look to book suppliers' areas of strength and match these to specific library needs. Librarians need to recognize that while the price of a title may be relatively constant, the value of the book to patrons may be time dependent. Librarians must work with suppliers to assure superior service levels to the library while generating sustaining profitability for the supplier. Articulation of library needs and honest, open communication with suppliers contributes to strong librarian-supplier relationships which ultimately yields superior service to the library and the patrons.

Establishing solid business relationships between librarians and suppliers is critical to the success of library collection development and acquisitions procedures. Librarians and suppliers share a partnership with the common objective of delivering quality service. The quality and timeliness of a supplier's service to a library has a direct relationship to the library's ability to deliver quality and timely service to patrons. This partnership between librarian and supplier begins with a clear understanding of the goals the librarian wants to achieve and suppliers' ability to respond to and meet those goals.

Although the basic concept of supplying books (and related materials) to libraries seems simple, the sheer numbers of titles and publishers involved quickly make this process complex. Add to this

Larry Price is Vice President and General Manager, Ingram Library Services Inc., 1125 Heil Quaker Blvd., La Vergne, TN 37086.

complexity the variety of special services librarians require and request and the seemingly simple process of supplying books to libraries becomes daunting.

In addition to the partnership suppliers share with librarians, suppliers also form a partnership with publishers. Since the vast majority of books sold to libraries are purchased through wholesalers, the quality of these partnerships becomes critical to the efficient and effective exchange of books and information. Increasingly librarians look to the supplier as a source for information about titles and their availability.

Publishers seek expanded information about the sales of their titles, what types of libraries purchased the titles, within what time frame, geographical patterns of sales, etc. The supplier becomes pivotal in this information exchange. It is reasonable to expect that this role for the supplier will intensify as publishers seek more efficient means of disseminating information about their titles.

Increasing costs of production and distribution of publishers' catalogs will force publishers to seek ways to control these expenses and to look for alternatives to present distribution methods, most commonly via mail using an in-house maintained database mailing list. Collection development librarians complain of the difficulty of getting publishers' catalogs and publishers express concern about their catalogs reaching the appropriate audience and getting used. Suppliers have an opportunity to use their partnerships to satisfy the needs of librarians and publishers in this information exchange.

LEVELS OF SERVICE

As librarians assess their satisfaction with suppliers, they must also examine their own needs and how these needs may be changing. The library community, as a market, has become more and more fragmented. No longer can suppliers treat libraries as a single customer base. Segmentation of the library market requires continual refining. Definition of these market segments may be based more on the service demands and expectations than on the client-base these libraries serve.

Librarians should review with suppliers changes not only to library collection development and acquisitions procedures but also changes to service expectations placed on the supplier. While the supplier may be capable of meeting heightened service expectations, enhanced services may require discount adjustments or separate invoices to recover the costs of these added services. Direct, open communication on a regular basis, whether initiated by the librarian or by the supplier, will help maintain a strong partnership and minimize misunderstandings.

In gaining an understanding of suppliers' services, librarians should determine the basic services offered, enhanced services which may be tied to specific programs such as approval plans on continuations services, and value-added services for which the supplier should expect to invoice additional charges.

After carefully determining the needs of the library, librarians should articulate their requirements to suppliers. Even in the absence of any existing specific service or program to satisfy these requirements, suppliers can frequently tailor their service by blending programs already available. By working as partners, librarians and suppliers can develop hybrid programs and services rather than developing new customized services. This, in turn, helps suppliers control cost and allows librarians to benefit from enhanced services sooner.

Exploring the library needs and suppliers' ability to meet those needs may point out the practicality of using more than one supplier and to select suppliers based on service strengths and capabilities. Just as the library market is fragmented, suppliers have tended to develop their services to target specific market segments. American business, in general, is becoming segment or niche oriented. It is not realistic to expect a single supplier to excel in all service areas for all market segments.

Libraries and suppliers operate in dynamic environments. Regular evaluation of service requirements and fulfillment is essential to the librarian-supplier partnership.

COLLECTION DEVELOPMENT SERVICES

The partnership between librarians and suppliers extends beyond the realm of acquisitions and into collection development and technical services. Librarians rely on supplier knowledge of publishing information to help make advanced collection development decisions.

Suppliers are eager to assist librarians in streamlining title selection and in providing librarians with the information they need to make informed buying decisions. By listening and responding to needs expressed by librarians, suppliers have developed an array of collection development programs and plans which can be adapted or even customized to the particular requirements of a specific library. Approval plans, continuations plans, and new title announcement programs are a few examples of these types of programs.

Most suppliers also produce regular catalogs to keep customers informed of new titles and to make title selection and ordering more convenient. Suppliers frequently distribute catalogs covering specific subjects of interest to collection development librarians.

As convenient as catalogs and particular collection development programs and plans may be, they do not always satisfy the individual projects collection development librarians may face. For example, if a librarian is concentrating on building the library's computer book collection, the supplier may be able to provide computer reports which are customized to meet the criteria of the project. In fact, suppliers can successfully work with librarians to analyze criteria for larger collection development projects and schedule production of the reports in an effort to keep the project manageable and the supplier reports timely.

Involving suppliers in collection development, as well as acquisitions, offers librarians the opportunity to tap into the collective knowledge the supplier has gained from working with other librarians and with publishers. In a sense, the supplier acts as a consultant who has a keen interest in the success of the library. Often, suppliers can present more efficient means to select and acquire titles without infringing on librarians' professional judgments.

The success of the librarian-supplier partnership in collection development demands trust and communication. Most suppliers employ librarians who are familiar with librarian expectations and who can interpret these expectations as deliverable services from the supplier. Working together the librarian and supplier can refine the library's requirements and adapt the supplier capabilities to satisfy those requirements.

TECHNOLOGY-BASED SERVICES

Library automation has created new challenges and opportunities for suppliers. Suppliers must be concerned not only with the development of the systems needed to run their businesses day to day, but must also be familiar with the variety of systems used by libraries.

As librarians seek ways to reduce or eliminate labor-intensive processes, they look to suppliers to provide information in machine-readable formats. Issues of standardization of data formats and hardware compatibility abound. Nevertheless, demand for electronic exchange of information will surely intensify. Librarians have embraced technology as a means of controlling personnel costs related to technical services and as a means of enhancing access to information.

Suppliers also recognize the value of technology in library technical services. Most suppliers offer PC-based electronic ordering programs to reduce order preparation time and improve order accuracy. Some suppliers are offering or developing services to electronically transfer packing list, invoice, and order/backorder status information. However, in all of these areas, the issue of standardization becomes critical to the development and ongoing support of such vendor-supplied information. The expense of developing multiple software programs to support the variety of library automation systems in place is staggering. Librarians and suppliers must again work as partners to determine the value of this information exchange and how the cost is to be recovered.

In addition to supplier-specific information, librarians are also turning to suppliers for the transfer or downloading of bibliographic records related to their book acquisitions. This generally is regarded as a value-added service and invoiced separately from the books provided.

Technology-based services create new partnerships for the librarian and the supplier, expanding beyond the supply of books which was the primary expectation. Frequently, technology-based services also bring additional parties into the librarian-suppliers partnership. The cooperation of library automation systems suppliers is critical to the success of technology-based services.

Librarians can readily examine invoices to determine the cost of the books and services they receive from suppliers. The value librarians receive in these transactions is much less tangible or concrete. After all, value is relative and is tied to a specific library's objectives and structure. Nevertheless, librarians must challenge and assess potential conflicts between cost and value. A book that is free, while having no cost attached to it, may also be of no value if there is no perceived potential use for the book.

One component of value is time. A bestseller which is published today at $22.95 will probably cost $22.95 in six months (assuming it is still in print and that the price has not increased). However, to many patrons the value has diminished after initial popularity for the title has waned and the title has lost its moment of fame on the bestseller list. And this time/value relationship is no longer unique to bestsellers. The timeliness of supplier service has value to the librarian. The timeliness of library processing of invoicing has value to supplier and may be reflected in discounts.

Suppliers operating on demand driven inventories of titles can offer prompt fulfillment of popular titles and competitive discounts. Suppliers offering approval plans operate on a different delivery cycle and cost structure. Both suppliers offer distinct cost and value opportunities for librarians.

Some supplier services may impact library costs. If a librarian can shift certain procedures or functions over to the supplier, an opportunity to reduce costs may result. Sometimes something as simple as the arrangement of the supplier packing list may affect the library's cost of receiving.

While supplier invoices may appear to give a solid indication of cost, librarians must question all aspects of cost and must also determine the value of the goods and service received.

CONSOLIDATION OF SUPPLIERS

During the 1980's the publishing industry underwent tremendous consolidation as publishers came under new ownership and management. It is reasonable to expect that the same will occur with library wholesalers in the 1990's.

As market conditions change and library service requirements intensify, some suppliers will lack the resources – financial, technological and people – to remain competitive. Some suppliers will look for opportunities to buy out other suppliers as a means of gaining necessary services, capabilities, or access to new market segments.

On the surface this consolidation of suppliers may appear disquieting to librarians. However, a positive result of this consolidation will likely be greater competition among fewer suppliers. This competition will become evident in the arenas of discount and value-added services. In addition, services will become more standardized. Librarians who have clearly identified the service requirements and expectations for their respective libraries will be prime beneficiaries.

As consolidation of suppliers occurs, librarians must be ready to exercise their partnership roles and to voice their needs. The relationships will continue to be people relationships, but adjustments to the changes caused by this consolidation will place new emphasis on established relationships. Avoidance to change will not alter its course, but may make the acceptance more difficult. Librarian-supplier partnerships will keep communication lines open for a better understanding of the affects change will have.

In the past decade, librarians have built partnerships with suppliers, albeit with some hesitation and suspicion. Perhaps the fundamental reason for this hesitation and suspicion is the difference by which librarians' and suppliers' results are measured. Librarians are measured on quantifiable data which tends to be elusive – circulation, patron use, etc. Suppliers are measured by profit – the bottom line.

It may be worth reconsidering the librarian-supplier partnership as being based on mutual success. The success of the supplier has a direct relationship to the success of the librarian. To achieve mutual success, both the librarian and the supplier must respect and communicate with one another.

Suppliers in the 1990's are interested in more than merely filling orders. Suppliers want to understand the problems librarians face and work toward realistic solutions. Librarians and suppliers must be prepared for change. By working together, as partners, librarians and suppliers can be ready for change and to put that change to advantage.

Librarians and suppliers have the opportunity to break down walls of resistance and hesitation. We have seen many librarians join the ranks of suppliers. This ultimately improves supplier responsiveness to librarians. Librarians must be bold in establishing their expectations for suppliers. Suppliers and librarians can then work together in achieving the goals librarians have set.

The 1990s—Is There Any Room Left?

Leonard Schrift

To many, in general, the world of libraries, publishing houses, and booksellers still reflects an ancient image of hushed voices, dust, and timelessness. The durability of this traditional image is quite ironic, considering the technological revolutions of the last two decades, and that even today this world is still in the midst of such elemental and profound processes that it would be totally unrecognizable to anyone harboring those old time-honored notions.

The process of change is so dramatic in its pace and complexity that any attempt to describe the state of the academic library or any component of its expanded world, namely publishers and library vendors, must assume the "frozen frame" approach. Such an approach however, as interesting as it may be, is not very useful in a predictive manner, as it ignores by definition, the fluidity and the dynamic interplay of the key elements in the process that brings about the very profound changes in the library world.

To be able to gain insight into the current state of affairs and, more importantly, to project developments into the future, it is incumbent upon us to identify and analyze the key elements that underlie the essential processes in the library related world, and to try to understand the ways they are likely to influence future developments. Undoubtedly the main force that will shape this world is the continuing conflict between expanding needs and contracting resources. This conflict not only affects supply and demand, but will impact all aspects of decision making, and certainly will determine the future shape of the library vending industry. In terms of the academic library's needs and demands, it is quite easy to see that

Leonard Schrift is President of Ballen Booksellers International, Inc., 125 Richfield Lane, Hauppauge, NY 11788.

29

both are destined to grow in a fast pace fueled by the ever growing demand for informational services in the research and academic community, and always by the new and fast changing technologies. The problem, however, is that this expansion of need occurs in a period of diminishing resources, which are crucially needed to finance this expansion. If one considers that this basic conflict is further aggravated by spiraling publisher prices of library materials, and by a serious reduction in the economic viability of the library service and support industry, it is easy to see that major structural changes and new "modus operandi" is in store.

Even today, it is practically impossible for me to think of a library that has "enough" money to meet its ideal materials acquisitions goals, its non-print information requirements, and its operational and support needs. There is absolutely nothing on the horizon to suggest any relief for this financial "straight jacket" in the foreseeable future. If anything, all government levels, from the federal through states and localities, are facing staggering budget deficits that mandate further reduction in support of research and higher education. Nor can the academic library community expect any relief in terms of the cost of material. The pricing record of the publishing industry since the 1970's is one of relentless annual price increases that have far outstripped the inflation rate in the economy. The unreasonableness of most price increases, especially in the price of periodicals, is familiar to and resented by the library community but has not yet resulted in any concerted and effective counter action that will deter the publishing industry's exploitative practices.

In its relating to the publishing industry, the library has been, and in many ways still is, an unwitting captive of the past. Although the publisher of old, the bibliophile for whom publishing was as much a mission as it was a business venture, has long been replaced by the ruthlessly efficient, "bottom line"-oriented corporate executive for whom a book is simply a product just like any other. Even though the publishing house, once inspired by letters and scholarship, is now just a subsidiary of a multi-national conglomerate with the same "profit center" responsibilities as any other division or product. Yet, many librarians still view the publisher as an ally, as a partner.

CHANGING FACE OF PUBLISHING

Not only is that nostalgic and romantic view of the publisher an anachronism, but the contemporary publishing environment is strongly affected by relatively recent developments, likely to bear tremendous additional pressure in the direction of higher prices and confusingly erratic publishing policies and practices. A primary area exerting such pressure is that a very important segment of scientific, technical, and medical publishing is done by publishers based outside the United States. This fact is of special significance as related to periodicals whose prices escalate in Dollar terms whenever the U.S. currency weakens vs. the European exchanges, and remain at their established high level when the Dollar gets stronger. This rather unfair and unjustified practice is possible because the demand for journal subscriptions is not flexible enough, and publishers can expect substantial increases in their revenue, despite a relatively low number of cancellations.

The second element, and in many ways more worrisome in its future adverse effects, is the recent wave of take-overs, both amicable and hostile. Only the distant future will tell if the buy-outs, mergers, and acquisitions result in any economic benefits of scale. Even so, there is no basis for an expectation that the publishers will pass any such benefit on to the library. What is more immediately clear and inevitable, is the tremendous financial pressure that leveraged buy-outs exert on the publishing companies. The immense financial obligations incurred in such acquisitions will cause a relentless pressure to increase cash flow and profits, which can come from only two sources, namely higher prices and curtailed operations. The negative effects of the higher prices are obvious. Those of curtailed operations are more subtle but in the long run just as damaging. Important scholarly works, which are marginal in terms of their profit potential, may simply no longer be published at all. One very sad aspect of the entire take-over activity is that their damage is inflicted whether successful or not. The same level of financial burden and debt service is assumed by the predator in his take-over bid, or by its target itself if successful in its struggle for survival.

Electronic technology has contributed in a major way to the operational efficiency of many libraries, enabling them to control growth in staffing levels while widening the scope and variety of user services. At the same time, the availability of new and capable technologies compelled them to invest ever growing amounts in their technological infrastructure. Unfortunately, there is nothing on the technology horizon to suggest any respite or financial relief. On the contrary, technology is likely to increase its burden on the library financial resources for many reasons, some real, some perceived.

It is quite clear that the pace of technological innovation has not yet abated. It will, in most likelihood, continue to accelerate. Prices of equipment have indeed come down, but only for older, less efficient, and less capable technology. The pre-obsolescence life of any new electronic technology has been remarkably short, compelling a relatively quick and costly replacement with the inherent danger that insufficient evaluation period may prove seemingly promising technologies to be expensive, "dead end" failures. Many libraries do get into this spiral of technology and costs because of the great desire to be at the forefront of technology, of the state of the art of the information science. In their eagerness many libraries lose sight of the fact that not being at the "cutting edge" does not mean being behind, that by allowing for a slower more deliberative technology adoption process they enable themselves to get into the right technological generation, to the mature, the tried and true, and the financially sensible state of professional sophistication.

The main negative impact from the financial standpoint is not so much the cost of the technology itself, but, rather, the cost of the information itself. It is so because it is the very same segment of the publishing industry that has always taken advantage of the library's inability to deny itself access to important information just because of extortive prices that still determines, controls, and regulates the access to the information and its cost.

BUDGETARY CONSTRAINTS

Although the library community is acutely aware of its financial predicament, it has not yet been able to identify its underlying causes and thus pursue those courses of action that would promise a more profound and long-term solution to its financial and budgetary problems. There is no doubt in my mind that eventually, after exhausting all other possible avenues, the library community will focus its energies and determination in the right direction. While the long-term solution can clearly be achieved only by a concerted community effort, it is the isolated, individual effort that characterizes libraries' struggle to find immediate relief.

The library vendor is the most immediate direction to which the library turns as the ready remedy when faced by pressing, yet conflicting needs of reducing costs, and enhancing service simultaneously. Obviously the vendor is not the element that determines the price of library material. The vendor, however, is the most direct and immediate contact of the library, it is the source to turn to for service, and therefore is in a weak economic position to resist pressures forcefully.

The general reduction in acquisitions funding puts a tremendous economic pressure on vendors even without direct library approaches for new concessions. As less money is available for buying material, many vendors react to weakening sales by desperate efforts to maintain sales levels and market share. In their eagerness to preserve their market position and sales volumes, many vendors compete fiercely by offering ever growing discounts to libraries. Many libraries do welcome this "price war" because it offers the appearance, short-term and false as it may be, of cost relief and reduction. Unfortunately, the fierce discounting phenomenon runs counter to all economic realities and as a result what may appear to be a price benefit will result in greater costs and difficulties to the library.

To begin with, the library service industry is an industry that operates at very slim profitability margins as can easily be demonstrated by the basic cost structure of the academic bookseller. Related to its total sales in terms of list prices, the basic cost of doing business is in the 19% - 23%. The main component of this cost element is, of course, the direct cost of labor, but its other components too are just as inflexible in terms of cost reduction and control:

- Statutory and Voluntary Employee Benefits.
- Space and Physical Facilities Costs.
- Utilities.
- Communications Costs.
- Computer Hardware and Other equipment.
- Freight Charges.
- Supplies.
- Travel and Meetings Costs.

These and other such operating costs are an inescapable part of doing business, they are always subject to upwards pressure, and they cannot be reduced meaningfully without an immediate parallel reduction in the level of provided service.

The revenue side of the equation is determined by the discounts granted booksellers by the publishers. The average such discount, in the case of the academic bookseller, falls within the range of 29% - 32%. The actual discount realized depends on three criteria:

a. The actual "mix" of orders in terms of type of material and publishing sources i.e., commercial publishers, esoteric publishers, societies, scholarly titles, "trade" titles, etc.
b. The bookseller's size as a buyer. Generally speaking, major booksellers benefit from a better negotiating position than smaller ones.
c. The bookseller's relative purchasing efficiency as determined by the ability to navigate in, and benefit from, the maze of terms, conditions, plans, arrangements, and special situations presented by a publishing universe of more than 40,000 sources.

The simple reality evident from this basic analysis is that the cost structure of our industry allows for an overall profit margin of only 6% - 13%. Considering that this rather slim margin should provide for both library's discount and bookseller's profit, it is easy to see that any excessive discount given by bookseller to library, whether for preserving market share or for any other reason, eliminates the viability of such a vendor as a going concern.

The economic picture of the bookseller cannot be considered static by any measure. The bookseller who has to cope with spiraling operating costs, by ever tightening managerial controls, is now faced with a clear worsening of discount and credit terms from a publishing industry saddled with debt service imperatives, resulting from speculative takeovers and fights for corporate survival. Squeezed by mounting costs on one hand and by shrinking revenues on the other, vendors will have to react by reducing levels and lowering standards of service. Unluckily, these service reductions will occur at the very time that the library is looking to the vendor to provide higher levels of service, at a lower price. The unfortunate result of this conflict will be the disappearance of many vendors through business failures, acquisitions, and mergers. From the standpoint of the library's situation, this chain of events will confirm the fallacy and shortsightedness of trying to find financial relief by relying on discounting. Although the vendor deals with a physical product, the product is not his and he has no control over its price. The nature of the vendor's business and ultimately its importance to the library, is the provision of service and it is the library, therefore, who pays the price for the vendor's crippled ability to provide the desired level of service.

BUYING DIRECTLY COSTS MORE

In their plight, some libraries try to reduce their acquisitions costs by ordering directly from publishers. This course of action, too, may appear to be reasonable and promising, while, in reality, its economies are false in the short-term and downright counter-productive in the long run. The proposition that buying directly at the source, bypassing the middleman would result in savings is very plausible at face value. The fallacy is rooted in the fact that by buying directly the library denies itself of the vendor's service contribution and must instead pay for the lost services itself, by assuming a myriad of small tasks and activities performed previously by the vendor. While by itself each aspect of such activities is immaterial, their cumulative cost far exceeds the apparent price savings. The long-term effect on prices is much more negative in its impact. Misled by libraries' interest in buying directly from them, publishers commit themselves to higher overhead costs and to high expenses of direct selling, travelling representatives, and the fulfillment costs of small orders. When they realize that their costs had gone up while their total sales remained essentially unchanged (as libraries do not buy more just because the purchase is direct), publishers would soon increase their prices in order to defray the new costs.

The learning process of trial and error is unfortunately slow and long. It is very costly, not only in monetary terms, but also because of the many casualties it will leave in the ranks of library service vendors. As is the case with all learning processes the eventual outcome will be positive and rewarding to the library. The library will have to assume a strategic approach to its problems and seek permanent solutions, rather than rely on "easy fixes," costly acquisitions practices disguised as "economies," or solutions that are "too good to be true." The library will realize again that the vendor is an ally and not an adversary, that being financially secure is very much to the library's advantage.

The changed library service industry will prove to be a worthy ally as well. The smaller number of vendors will be composed of the hardy survivors of the currently adverse market conditions. The survivors will be those firms that are well managed, financially sound, technologically able, and with a diversity of markets. The survivors will be able to offer a wide range of services at the very same time that libraries will again emphasize the importance of service, in all of its obvious and subtle aspects.

Faced with a library community armed with commonality of purpose and focused in its determination and efforts, the publishing industry too will have to rethink its structure and attitudes. A failure in becoming truly responsive to the library (and academic community) needs and concerns, is likely to result in alternative publishing methods. Emerging technologies will provide a technological foundation to academic self-publishing enterprises, based on the fact that the academic community is the originator and the source of the very same knowledge that is the raw material of today's publishing industry.

The conclusion, stated very simply, is that there still remains many more questions than there are answers. More questions that have satisfactory answers to them seem to prompt at least two more non-answerable questions. Where do we go from here?

SELECTION AND EVALUATION OF VENDORS – THE LIBRARIAN SPEAKS . . .

A Method for Evaluating Vendor Performance

Charles W. Brownson

SUMMARY. The probability that a firm order will be satisfied is highest in the first months after ordering and decreases the longer the order remains open. This probability can be described mathematically. A method of obtaining such a function is explained, and its uses examined: in evaluating the performance of competing vendors, in analyzing regional or temporal receipt patterns, in predicting receipts to determine the optimum cancellation time, and in predicting costs to control encumbrances.

Experience with library acquisitions suggests that, of a group of orders all placed at the same time, most will be filled in the first months, with fewer and fewer supplied as time goes by. Some orders will never be filled at all. Experience also suggests that this

Charles W. Brownson is Humanities Co-ordinator, Collection Development, Arizona State University Libraries, Tempe, AZ 85287.

pattern of fulfillment is fairly regular; regular enough, perhaps, to be described mathematically.

One can see at once some possible uses for a mathematical expression which would describe the probability of fulfillment as a function of the age of an order. In particular, vendor performance could be described on a more precise basis using such a method. Vendors who fill orders quickly might seem preferable, but perhaps not if the overall fulfillment rate is low. Conversely, a relatively slow vendor who is nevertheless able to handle esoteric or scarce titles might be preferable in other cases. Vendors acquire reputations which experienced librarians know and use in matching orders to vendors. A mathematical function which analyzes both speed and total performance would enable the working librarian to verify this intuitive knowledge, and also to evaluate new vendors in the absence of experience.

This question has been thoroughly investigated in a recent article by Michael Cooper.[1] Cooper explains variation in receipt pattern by models able to predict arrival probability and also analyze the contribution of particular hazards such as imprint age, subject, and country of origin to the overall failure rate. Cooper's discoveries suggest the possibility of a simplified analysis, of the nature of a diagnostic probe which could be easily computed and routinely used to identify and focus problems either for heuristic attack or for more thorough analysis.

Consider the fate of orders placed during one month, in this case 579 orders placed during September, 1987 (Table 1). Nine of these orders were filled in September, 87 more in the second month following the order (that is, during October), and 181 in the third month. After November, successive months produce fewer fulfillments, settling down to a steady trickle, so that of the original 579 orders have been filled. Half the orders, however, were filled in the first three months, and two-thirds in the first five months. This is the pattern expected.

With no other information, and in particular without inquiring into the reasons for which orders went unfilled, might it be possible to construct a useful diagnostic tool?

If we express each successive month's receipts as a percent of the total number of orders placed, a graph of the partial sums of these

TABLE 1. English language firm orders placed in September 1987 – Receipts in successive months following ordering

Month	Titles recd	Cum	Pct	Cum pct
1	9	9	1.55	1.55
2	78	87	13.47	15.03
3	181	268	31.26	46.29
4	75	343	12.95	59.24
5	34	377	5.87	65.11
6	29	406	5.01	70.12
7	8	414	1.38	71.50
8	6	420	1.04	72.54
9	7	427	1.21	73.75
10	4	431	0.69	74.44
11	3	434	0.52	74.96
12	10	444	1.73	76.68

Total orders placed: 579

percents (that is, the cumulative percent received by the end of each succeeding month) will be a curve which rises quickly and tails off to the right. Such a curve might be described by an expression of the form $y = a - f(x)$, where y is the percent of orders filled up to month x; the curve is described as a function of x which approaches (from below) a constant value a, which is the maximum number of orders that will ultimately be fulfilled. The value of f(x) grows, but more and more slowly, with the value of x; that is, with the increasing age of the order. This pattern is characteristic of all growth, and a typical such function is b/x^c; the constant b is divided by the value of x raised to the power of c.

The fit of this expression ($y = a - b/x^c$) can be tested by regression analysis, and the values of the constants (a, b, c) determined. However, the method of linear regression requires an expression without exponents (x^c) and of the form $y = bx + a$. An expression of the requisite form can be obtained by substituting for x in the linear equation, the value of the function $1/x^c$. Linear regression then produces the values of a and b; using these parameters, a range of values for c can be tested to find one which produces the best fit (as measured by the coefficient of correlation r).

This is a straightforward procedure when applied to a single cohort (a batch of orders all placed at the same time) which is old enough for the fate of all the orders in the cohort to be known. This is not a practical requirement. Ordinarily we would want to analyze data of mixed cohorts: orders placed at different times, some too recent for their fates to be definitively known. The simplest way to proceed would be to sum all the data in a single series. Let us suppose 20,000 orders placed during the last two years. Of these, 400 are twenty or more months old. Most of these 400 will have been fulfilled long ago, two orders were fulfilled in the twentieth month, and a few orders are still open. Thus, 0.5% (2/400) of the eligible orders were filled in the twentieth month. In the case of the tenth month, more orders are eligible, and all 20,000 are included in the calculations for the first month, all of them having had a chance to be filled in that amount of time. Thus, if 300 orders are found to have been filled in less than a full month from the date of order, then 1.5% (300/20,000) of the eligible orders were filled in the first month.

DATA ANALYSIS

However, a library does not place and receive orders uniformly the year round. At some points in the fiscal cycle there will be many new unfilled orders, while at other times there will be relatively few new orders and many old ones, most of them now closed (that is, for titles already received). The analysis is likely to give very different results in these cases. The solution is to regress each monthly cohort separately and derive a representative curve from the results by a second regression.

Thirty months of data from a single university library were analyzed by this means to produce the curve shown in Figure 1. This particular curve has the expression $y = 91.06 - 97.73/x^{0.89}$, where x is the month of receipt and y is the total percent of orders fulfilled by the end of that month. This curve approaches a line having a value given by the parameter a = 91.06, but the actual proportion of orders which will eventually be filled is somewhat less; even at 500 months the value of y has reached only 90.68, and very few orders are likely to be left open 500 months. Thus, the results indicate that the library can expect to fill no more than about 90% of its orders. The first orders will be filled in just over a month (the curve

FIGURE 1. Probability of order fulfillment

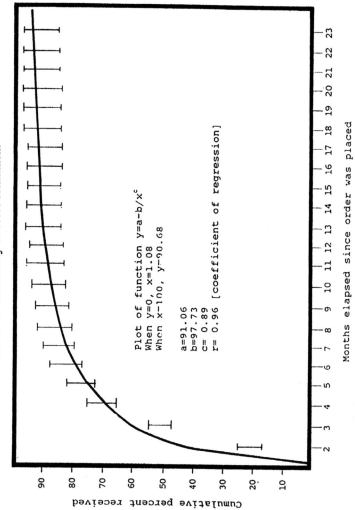

Plot of function $y=a-b/x^c$
When $y=0$, $x=1.08$
When $x=100$, $y=90.68$

a=91.06
b=97.73
c= 0.89
r= 0.96 [coefficient of regression]

Months elapsed since order was placed

Cumulative percent received

crosses the x axis at 1.08) and most of the ultimately successful orders will have been filled in the first seven months and nearly all in the first year.

This function also characterizes the alacrity with which a vendor is able to fill orders. A slower rate of response shows up as a flatter curve (leaning more to the right) which is measured by a combination of the parameters b and c. However, in all the analyses performed so far the value of c has not been observed to vary from 0.89 for firm order vendors, so that we may say that the smaller the value of b the steeper the curve. The parameter b is simply a number, similar in intent to average response time but lacking an intuitive equivalent. It is more accurately descriptive than an average, however, being much less sensitive to distortion by outliers (those few orders filled with unusual promptness or very slowly).

The point at which the first orders are received (the point where the curve crosses the x axis) varies only slightly (the range observed is 1.02 to 1.15) and is not of much interest in evaluating the rate of response.

This function describes the data quite well, having a coefficient of correlation of 0.958. However, its parameters are undoubtedly sensitive to variations between libraries and must be locally calibrated with a suitably large and representative set of local data before using it as a diagnostic tool.

Now we are in a position to evaluate vendor performance using this function. When the parameters a and b are calculated using the orders placed with a single vendor, we may say that any vendor having a value of a > 91.06 is more successful than the average for this library and any vendor having a value of b < 97.73 is quicker overall at filling orders. As between vendors, we will look for one which maximizes the one parameter (a) and minimizes the other (b).

It would also be possible to use this function to describe the receipt pattern characteristic of a region or a particular time in the publishing cycle. How much better is the library (if it is better) at obtaining domestic publications, for example, than at obtaining British or French ones? Given the (presumably) higher expectations for prompt and complete fulfillment of orders for domestic publications, how do the library's domestic vendors compare to its foreign ones?

An analysis of this sort is presented in Table 2. Here we see that this library's particular mix of French vendors are quicker at filling orders than European vendors as a whole (104 vs. 108) but not quite as effective overall (94 vs. 98); the German vendors, by contrast, are slower but ultimately fill more orders. This might be attributed to a difference in the publishing environments of the two countries (books going out of print faster in France, perhaps) or it might really be characteristic of the vendors themselves.[2] Such a difference might also result from the way a library uses a particular vendor. Vendor #1, for example, has a high fulfillment rate (101.9) but is fairly slow (112 vs. the average of 97 for English-language titles). However, the orders which this library gives to vendor #1, firm orders for titles not supplied by the library's domestic approval plans, tend to be older imprints as well as more esoteric. Given these conditions, the performance of vendor #1 might be expected to be slower than the average. A thoroughgoing evaluation of competing vendors would compare their performance on material presenting the same procurement problems. Such a comparison may be seen in the differences between vendor #1 and vendor #2, which receives a high proportion of more difficult orders for titles not supplied by the library's routine British sources. Vendor #2 is

TABLE 2. Receipt pattern for some regions and vendors

Receipt source	limit	b	r	a	titles
All foreign vendors	99.22	116.3	0.93	99.68	912
Oriental vendors	98.45	125.1	0.90	98.94	419
Chinese vendors	88.78	104.9	0.82	89.20	18
Japanese vendors	98.89	126.4	0.90	99.39	401
European vendors	98.15	108.2	0.94	98.58	444
French vendors	94.57	104.2	0.92	94.99	223
German vendors	105.0	115.6	0.94	105.5	164
Italian vendors	92.00	137.5	0.79	92.54	62
Spanish language	94.54	89.24	0.97	94.89	49
English language	93.95	97.28	0.98	94.33	3958
Vendor #1 [US]	101.9	112.3	0.96	102.3	1719
Vendor #2 [UK]	88.95	103.8	0.95	89.36	793
All vendors Sep 1988	94.02	99.18	0.97	94.41	4870
Average FY 1988/89	90.68	97.73	0.96	91.06	

For the function $y = a - b/x^c$; $c = 0.89$
Spanish language combines Spanish and Latin American vendors.
English language combines US, Canadian, and British vendors.

faster than the domestic vendor #1 (indeed, faster than all the European and Oriental vendors) but fills somewhat fewer orders.

TRADEOFFS AND OBSERVATIONS

This initial comparison between vendors #1 and #2 suggests there may be something of a tradeoff between speed and effectiveness, a suggestion which has some intuitive support. Vendors emphasizing speed are less likely to continue to search for unprofitable material, whereas vendors emphasizing effectiveness are likely to keep a big backlog of unfilled orders. The function described here offers a means of verifying this intuitive knowledge and of measuring the differences between vendors.

The data in Table 2 suggests several other observations. Firstly, in the case of German receipts, and also those from vendor #1, the ultimate success might appear to be above 100%. However, it should be remembered that this parameter (a) is only a number measuring the height of the curve. In actuality, 98% of German orders and 96% of orders to vendor #1 will be filled by the twenty-fourth month, the maximum realistic age for an order to be left unfilled. Secondly, the paucity of data for Italian and Chinese orders is reflected in lower correlations, which underlines the statistical nature of this evaluative tool, which cannot be used on small vendors or other data sets of less than one or two hundred cases. The analysis for Spanish-language receipts, although correlated adequately with the data, should thus perhaps not be trusted, since the small size of the data set suggests the analysis may not be very representative. Thirdly, as has been pointed out above in the case of vendor #1, this technique cannot be used independently of all that is known about factors affecting vendor performance. For Chinese vendors, for example, the correlation is driven down by the vendors' habit of batching orders and filling them at intervals of more than a month to save on shipping costs, so that even if the data set were larger the correlation might not rise.

In general, however, I believe it may be said that this function does demonstrate a substantial regularity in the receipt of library firm orders, which would appear to be, in the aggregate at least, highly predictable. The particular function derived here performs realistically, though it over-estimates early receipts, as can be readily seen in Figure 1. Possibly a more sophisticated analysis would discover a curve which fits the data better than this one discovered by linear regression. It is also possible that data from other libraries, particularly much larger or smaller libraries, might show a different, perhaps substantially different, pattern.

A number of corollary uses for this technique will come to the reader's mind in addition to the one discussed so far, of analyzing vendor performance. One obvious use would be to determine the optimum cancellation time. For this library the optimum time would appear to be after thirteen months, by which time all but a few percent (about 100 titles) have been supplied of those which ultimately will be supplied. Both vendors #1 and #2, being slower than average, require a bit more time to realize their potential. Vendor #2, only a bit slower and about as effective as the average, requires fifteen months to reach the norm in effectiveness, while vendor #1, being significantly slower, should be given eighteen months.

Optimizing vendor selection and cancellation time would work to improve the overall effectiveness of the Acquisitions Department, which could also be measured by this function. The effect of optimizing efforts should be reflected in changes in the function's parameters, with more orders filled (increasing parameter a), and filled more quickly (decreasing parameter b).

So far we have examined only firm orders, but this method could also be used to evaluate approval plan vendors. If we knew the total number of titles which the library would like to have received on approval (a list which could perhaps be assembled from a competing vendor's list of titles supplied), then effectiveness could be measured by the proportion of titles actually supplied and speed by the time after publication required to supply them.

A list of engineering books published during the summer of 1989 was assembled by this means as a trial. The list was first pared to remove titles which were ultimately supplied from sources other than the vendor to be tested. These are titles for which the target vendor was excluded from the competition: foreign titles given to other vendors, society publications obtained directly from the publisher, and similar materials on which the target vendor should not be evaluated. Of the remaining 180 items, 59 had to be set aside because the publication date was unknown; these included 30 titles supplied by the target vendor. Of the 121 titles analyzed, 76 were ultimately supplied by the target vendor and 45 were not purchased by the library from any source. Most of the unpurchased titles were legitimately excluded by the target vendor as unwanted; that is, not within the scope of the approval plan profile. For this set of titles the projected month of publication was obtained from *Forthcoming Books* and the date of receipt was obtained from the library's records.

Regressing this data produces the equation $y = 72.37 - 143.7/x^{1.11}$, with a co-efficient of correlation $r = 0.984$.

THE VENDOR'S ULTIMATE SUCCESS

If one compares these parameters with those derived for firm order vendors, this approval vendor would seem quite slow and inefficient. This would be an unwarranted inference. Firstly, the vendor's ultimate success ($a = 72.37$) was evaluated against the universe of engineering books, insofar as the competing vendor who supplied the original list knows what the universe is. If one excludes the titles which the library never intended to buy and which were legitimately declared by the vendor to be out of scope, then the vendor's success will be shown to be nearly perfect. For purposes of this analysis it was also thought interesting to know that the library buys about two-thirds of the engineering titles which might be expected to be seriously considered for purchase by an academic library, which is the information obtained from parameter (a).

The parameters $b = 143.7$ and $c = 1.11$ measure in this case the combined performance of the vendor, the publisher in supplying the vendor, and also the publisher in meeting his own announced publication date. The library will receive its first books in a little under two months after projected publication and will receive most within ten months, but this analysis does not reveal how much of the delay can be attributed to the vendor. Presumably all approval vendors face similar constraints, but some may be more effective in obtaining prompt supply from publishers, so an attempt to separate these factors will hide some aspects of vendor performance. The caveat that this analysis measures performance under different conditions than those under which a firm order vendor works is underlined by the change in the parameter (c), which for firm order vendors was never observed to vary from a value of 0.89. To complete the analysis with a judgement on the adequacy of this particular approval the vendor would require data from another library showing the performance of a competing vendor on the same list of titles.

It is also possible to use the performance measure described in this paper to assess the early returns on a group of firm orders. Table 3 shows the combined performance of all firm orders month by month. Thus, for the period from July 1988 through April 1989, the library filled roughly 38% of its firm orders one or two months old; the range is from a low of 34.6% in April to a high of 40.9% in July. For orders up to three months old the library filled somewhat more than half during the period under scrutiny.

There is a reassuring regularity here, but even so, one can see that January and April receipts were lower for orders of all ages. If we examine the individual cohorts (Table 4) we see at once that third-month receipts for November orders were low (only 14% compared to the more usual 30%), and also fourth-month receipts for January orders (4% as against the usual 15%). This accounts for the reduced January and April receipts, January being the third month following November ordering and April the fourth after January. Scrutiny of the November and April orders might reveal the cause. Perhaps a new vendor was tried out, or a familiar vendor tried out on a new type of material. This analysis could be used to focus the diagnosis on a smaller, more manageable group of orders.

TABLE 3. Receipts from all orders during fiscal 1988/89 — Cumulative percent, orders received after less than six months

Mon	Jul	Aug	Sep	Oct	Nov	Dec	Jan	Feb	Mar	Apr
2	40.93	40.31	39.02	38.36	39.80	38.45	36.67	36.62	36.06	34.64
3	57.39	56.68	55.14	54.41	56.60	54.86	51.91	52.32	51.61	49.68
4	65.94	65.19	63.52	62.75	65.33	63.39	59.98	60.49	59.69	57.49
5	71.22	70.45	68.70	67.90	70.72	68.65	64.97	65.53	64.67	62.32

The month of receipt is given at the head of each column. So, for example, for titles received in July, 65.94% had been ordered in the last four months.

TABLE 4. Receipts from selected cohorts, fiscal 1988/89 in months 2-5 following order

	Pct received in month				Cum pct received		
	2	3	4	5	3	4	5
Sep	11.93	37.91	14.60	2.22	49.84	64.44	66.66
Oct	16.86	26.69	13.98	10.34	43.55	57.53	57.87
Nov	6.00	14.34	19.39	3.66	20.34	39.73	43.39
Dec	4.14	39.88	16.10	3.22	44.02	60.12	63.34
Jan	8.98	36.06	4.42		45.04	49.46	

The month of order is given in the left-hand column. So, for example, for titles ordered in September, 14.6% were received in the fourth month following and 64.44% were received by the fourth month (i.e., December).

More importantly, it demonstrates that it is not necessary to wait a year or two years for all the returns to come in before a vendor's performance can be given a preliminary analysis.

With only a few months' data we cannot, however, obtain the diagnosis directly from the parameters as we did in the first example. This is because the pattern of receipt in the early months is more complex than this relatively simple function $(a - b/x^c)$ is able to describe, as a glance at Figure 1 will show. An analysis which produced a curve better fitting the pattern of the earliest filled orders would be repaid by a simplified diagnosis of vendor performance in the crucial four to five months following the order.

BUDGET QUESTIONS

Most libraries which need to close their books at the end of a fiscal year do so by over-encumbering the budget to allow for uncertainty. Beginning the fiscal year with too much of the budget encumbered, however, mortgages the future. One survey revealed an average 28% encumbrance at the start of the fiscal year, four percent above what was considered acceptable.[3] In theory, the analysis of receipt pattern could assist in setting and monitoring the level of encumbrance. An example is given in Table 5. In this case, on May 1st one may expect to spend, before the end of the fiscal year, $70,417 plus 14% of the value of the May orders and 2% of the value of the June orders. Table 5 shows that the budget for the

TABLE 5. Predicted cost of receipts during the last two months of the fiscal year and during the next fiscal year, as of May 1st

Order date	Tot ord	Still open 5/01	Avg cost	Prob. rect <6/30	No. of titles expected	Prob. cost	Prob. rect next yr	No. of titles expected	Prob. cost
<Aug	5909	819	$34.05	.00	3	$102.15	.00	2	$82.69
Aug	552	100	$42.03	.03	3	$115.80	.02	2	$78.08
Sep	1951	501	$33.43	.03	15	$505.36	.03	14	$471.00
Oct	1540	385	$31.74	.04	16	$519.76	.03	13	$421.85
Nov	1530	799	$34.30	.07	58	$2,009.24	.04	35	$1,214.18
Dec	652	238	$47.09	.11	27	$1,275.04	.06	13	$1,275.04
Jan	746	377	$39.33	.26	100	$3,920.18	.07	27	$620.84
Feb	531	408	$31.85	.51	207	$6,581.31	.11	45	$1,077.56
Mar	1999	1850	$29.39	.58	1064	$31,266.64	.16	303	$8,904.95
Apr	1892	1891	$29.90	.43	807	$24,121.79	.33	624	$18,648.01
May				.14			.61		
Jun				.02			.72		
TOT	17302	7368			2300	$70,417.26		1080	$32,962.17

next fiscal year will require, to cover costs incurred in the previous year, $32,962 plus 61% of the value of the May orders and 72% of the value of the June orders. Now it is possible to calculate, given predictions concerning the next fiscal year's budget and the probable volume of ordering during May and June, what the value of encumbrances will be at the beginning of the year. In this case, the answer is about 15%, or well within norms.

The cost of orders filled during a particular month cannot be predicted so correctly, however, as Table 6 shows. In this test, the mathematical formula was supplemented by a cruder and less general method, that of extrapolating from previous receipts of the same age. This requires a good deal more data but better describes receipts in the first months following ordering, as a comparison of predicted August receipts for orders placed in May through July shows. The formula predicts 45 receipts, whereas the more empirical method predicts 54, and this discrepancy in the first three months is almost the whole discrepancy between the two methods. Neither method comes very close to predicting the 105 titles actually received in August, however. A regular pattern of receipts appears when observed over a substantial fraction of the possible life of the order, or six months to a year for firm orders which might be expected to remain open two years. Over shorter periods this regu-

TABLE 6. Actual vs. predicted receipts during August 1989

Month order	Predict A	B	Act ual	--Average cost-- predict	actual	--Predicted cost--- Method A	Method B	Actual cost
Aug	0	0	2	$26.42	$31.89	$.00	$.00	$63.79
Sep	1	1	11	$21.73	$21.85	$21.73	$21.73	$240.37
Oct	2	2	4	$22.95	$17.55	$45.90	$45.90	$70.20
Nov	3	1	4	$25.33	$39.15	$75.99	$25.33	$156.61
Dec	1	1	5	$47.64	$236.66	$47.64	$47.64	$1,183.34
Jan	0	0	1	$18.07	$21.46	$.00	$.00	$21.46
Feb	0	1	5	$30.01	$4.09	$.00	$30.01	$20.45
Mar	3	3	25	$52.33	$85.53	$156.99	$156.99	$2,138.39
Apr	2	2	13	$79.23	$82.10	$158.46	$158.46	$1,067.31
May	2	5	12	$26.38	$31.08	$52.76	$131.90	$373.04
Jun	26	42	20	$42.81	$67.99	$1,113.06	$1,798.02	$1,359.94
Jul	17	7	3	$5.69	$48.81	$96.73	$39.83	$244.05
TOTAL	57	65	105	$31.14	$64.85	$1,769.26	$2,455.81	$6,938.95

Method A: calculation using the function $y=a-b/x^c$
Method B: by extrapolation from actual receipts

larity is swamped by the innate variability of the data, made visible in Figure 1 by the vertical spread of the plotted observations. This variability is exacerbated by a much greater unpredictability in the cost of individual titles, which can be anything from free to thousands of dollars. As with the number of receipts, the cost of library materials is predictable in the aggregate only. Thus we see that, while August receipts were predicted to number about 60, costing about $31 each, in actuality 105 titles costing an average of $64.85 were received, for a total cost almost three times that predicted.

However, this comparison of predicted and actual costs does enable us to estimate the error attributable to the function's relatively poor modeling of the first three months' receipts. This error is only about 6%, which is the amount of the difference between receipts as predicted by the function $y = a - b/x^c$ (method A) and by extrapolation from actual receipts (method B).

The purpose of this investigation was to construct a diagnostic tool which is easily computed and would facilitate vendor comparisons and provide insight into other performance-related issues such as claiming and fiscal management. The proposed method has been shown to be both realistic and practical in such cases.

REFERENCES

1. Michael D. Cooper, "Modeling Arrival Patterns Of Library Book Orders." *Library and Information Science Research* 10 (1988) 237-255.

2. Cooper's analysis reveals a similar pattern and supports the suggestion that it is inherent in French publishing and distribution, not in the performance of a particular vendor (Cooper 246-247, 253).

3. *Library Acquisition Survey.* (Scranton: University of Scranton, Center For Book Research, 1985) 14.

Trends Affecting Vendor Selection: One Academic Library's Experience

Twyla Mueller Racz
Trudie A. Root

SUMMARY. This paper discusses a medium sized academic library's decision to consolidate its subscriptions with one periodical vendor and the trends that influenced this decision: library automation, greater emphasis on collection development, increased sophistication of agents' services, and rising serial costs. While noting the pros and cons of agent use, the reluctance of librarians to just use one vendor, the historical development of subscription agencies, as well as criteria for vendor selection, this paper emphasizes the benefits achieved for the library in terms of collection management including, budgeting and formula allocation, automation, and serials acquisitions work. Such a description will hopefully assist other librarians to reach a conclusion.

Rutledge and Swindler quote a German proverb, "Whoever has the choice, also has the misery,"[1] that still very aptly describes the problems librarians confront in dealing with the world of serials. In the past, many academic libraries including our own, placed more emphasis on monograph acquisitions than on serial purchases, even though the greater part of the materials budget was expended upon serials, and they were more costly in terms of handling, claiming, and binding. Our subscription list of approximately 4000 titles was automatically renewed year after year with a review only taking place in order to decide on which new titles to add. Cancellations were few until the late 70s and early 80s when the acquisitions

---

Twyla Mueller Racz is Coordinator, Collection Development, and Trudie A. Root is Serials Librarian, Learning Resources & Technologies, Eastern Michigan University, Ypsilanti, MI 48197.

budget was either reduced or remained static, and double-digit inflation hit. When the serials budget exceeded 75% of the total materials budget, the subscription and standing order lists were scrutinized for deletion possibilities. Duplicate titles, a few foreign titles, several very expensive titles, and some little-used titles were eliminated until the budget was in line again.

Today the proliferation of journal titles and the enormous rise in subscription costs, especially in the scientific fields, continue to impact the library's acquisitions budget. The tug-of-war between serials and monographs for a share in the budget has accelerated. When CD-ROM and other electronic technologies are added, the conflict worsens, and even greater stress is placed on the budget. Unfortunately, despite what the literature may lead us to believe, libraries will need to continue to collect serials. As of yet no electronic technology has completely replaced serial titles, although ABI INFORM comes the closest. In 1989, *American Libraries* reported the results of two meetings of librarians, publishers, and scholars on, "Will the printed scholarly journal last, and what's in store for the research library in the U.S.?"[2] Both agreed that the printed journal will remain. Since electronic options will not replace the journals in the near future, libraries must face reality and plan better to reduce acquisition costs.

How can these costs be reduced or contained? This becomes a compelling issue for collection management especially in light of Magrill's words

> . . . academic libraries have faced the increased visibility of their operations to college and university administrators and the expectations of these administrators that librarians will engage in businesslike planning and reporting.[3]

Libraries must gain control over serials. If they have chosen good subscription agents, help can be obtained from these agents through their automated management reports. Reports can be generated by subject, department, discipline, etc. Within each requested category the titles and their prices will be arranged by LC class letters. The lists can also be obtained in descending price order. Both types of reports are useful in assessing under- or over-expenditures, and in reviewing for possible deselections. Historical and current information on the percentage of price increases are also available. In addition, agents will advise libraries of the projected percentage increase for the coming year, thus providing the library with documentation that enables it to make better collection management decisions.

ONE AGENT OR SEVERAL AGENTS

The question of whether to use several agents or use one agent has fostered much discussion in the literature. Kuntz mentioned that with one agent, "there is less confusion and more economy."[4] However, he noted that libraries are unwilling to grant their titles to one vendor as they feel few agents can or will provide all of the titles. Libraries indicate that it is not good business practice to side with one agent. Kuntz countered this with the conclusion that "splitting the list lessens the advantages of using an agent and the customer with the larger account usually receives better service."[5] A more reasonable criterion for splitting one's list is the dollar amount or the mix of titles from high discount or low discount; using vendors in terms of geography and area of specialization were not favored by Kuntz as rationale for multiple agents.

In discussing the evolution of subscription agencies, Derthick and Moran noted that over the past ten or fifteen years there has been a reduction in the number of serial agencies, and that this trend, together with the increased computer capabilities of the large agents, has provided a "strong incentive for libraries to use fewer agents."[6] In a survey of ACRL libraries, Derthick and Moran found that on the average libraries employed 17 agents and 99% used more than one agent. When asked if libraries would like to use more, fewer, or the same number of agents, 44% said they wished to use fewer and only 9% said that they would like to use more agents. Forty-seven percent were satisfied with the current number of agents used. Reasons given for more agents included: libraries wanted to "try better services, encourage competition by splitting their business, and find more reliable agents in developing countries." Libraries desiring fewer agents cited that they wanted to "simplify routines and consolidate workflow, possibly obtain a lower service charge, take advantage of automation, and phase out poor performance agents.''[7]

Other writers such as Schmidt mentioned that there is little difference between the few competing subscription agencies and thus it is hard to know if changing vendors would be worthwhile. Moreover, large libraries may find switching vendors such an enormous task that they are kept from doing so.[8] ''Buzzy'' Basch explained how the subscription agencies are similar:

> All offer order placement; internal automation; consolidated payment, administration and claiming; online access to files of bibliographic and publisher information, reports and invoices customized to client needs; access to historic price data; machine readable data for local system input; generation of kardex labels; and the use of toll free telephone lines, and other additional services.[9]

Basch recommended examining the library's specific needs and the services that each agency offers to meet these needs.

Sanders noted that reports received from their major agent were less useful for collection development than they expected, as the list represented too small a percent of their titles. Sanders also made the following observations: the library tries to use the agent to do something the agent is not set up to do, such as order out of the area of specialization, and, the library may be dealing with too many agencies.

> Using multiple agencies becomes a problem when agency coverage overlaps and library orders are split between agents who offer essentially the same services. If nothing else the fact that each agency has its own special forms, its own online systems and its own special requirements the library must keep track of would mitigate against order splitting. Add to this the fact that service improves if the librarian works consistently with the same individual who becomes familiar with the library's needs, etc., and that service fees can be reduced for large orders, there seems little reason to maintain split orders.[10]

LIBRARIES THAT HAVE EXPERIENCED CONVERSION

In terms of the literature regarding conversion of subscription orders to fewer or to single agents, there are few articles providing information. Dora New discussed the transfer of 2800 serial titles obtained from several agents and publishers to one major agent at the University of California, Irvine. Before the transfer the serials department used 92 agents for their 5800 titles. She listed the following guidelines to help in the conversion process:

1. Plan well in advance.
2. Involve the staff.
3. Develop guidelines so that you have a fixed idea of what you want to do.
4. If possible, begin with an accurate base of information.
5. Choose your agent carefully.
6. After a period of time evaluate the new agent's performance.[11]

Dora New also added a vendor questionnaire for assistance.

In 1986 Anderson discussed order consolidation of 4600 titles from three vendors to one at Utah State University. Anderson attributed the success of their consolidation to the informal survey of libraries which had already consolidated orders, a Request for Proposal that was designed and sent to six vendors capable of supplying over 100,000 serial titles, and to the formal telephone survey of libraries currently using the proposed vendors regarding collection size, vendor service charge rate, and service satisfaction. A committee then quantified the evaluations using a score sheet, made the final decision to consolidate, and selected the vendor.[12]

CONSOLIDATION OF ORDERS

In 1988, certain events and facts led our library staff involved with serials to explore the desirability and options for vendor consolidation. Of importance to the library was the fact that planning had recently begun for implementation of the NOTIS integrated library system. After reading the documentation it was evident that it was prudent to consolidate before serials acquisitions was implemented, and, that in doing so, the library could take advantage of the agent's capabilities of sending invoices via a tapeload. Second, after reviewing the mix of titles for our library, which serves a medium sized university, it was clear that a major domestic agent could handle our titles; and, a separate overseas vendor was not necessary because most of our foreign titles were in English. Third, we were using two domestic agents providing similar services.

Also important was the fact that our acquisitions budget needed to be carefully monitored to prevent more money from being eroded from the monograph side. At the time funds were not available for ordering new serial titles, and, thus no new titles were ordered unless other titles were cancelled. Therefore, a review of our titles could more easily take place if the library could take advantage of the management report capabilities of major vendors. Reports would be more useful if all of our titles were included. Last, it would be beneficial if the service charge could be reduced.

Review of our vendors began. Vendor literature was examined for each of the major serial vendors in order to compare services and products. Our sales representatives had also recently visited our library, providing us with up-to-date information on their companies as well; we reread this information. Since we were currently using the two leading U.S. domestic agents, we compared service charges and prices for like titles. In addition, past claim activity, ordering success, forms used, and service provided by our service representatives were considered.

As our overseas vendor was found not to be needed, our decision rested between the two leading domestic agents. After comparisons were made, we decided to go with the vendor that had the majority of our titles. The main reasons for our final selection included the superior service we had been receiving from our client representative, a lower service charge as far as we could determine, the computer capabilities which suited our needs, and the clearer invoice and report forms.

With our decision to consolidate made, we proceeded to check that all of our titles were listed in the vendor catalog. For those that were not, we called our agent and received confirmation that all but a very few could be supplied. To expedite the process, our agent was very helpful in allowing us to utilize copies of the other agents' invoices which already had listed the expiration dates or volumes covered. We then added the vendor title numbers from our agent's catalog as well as the subject and division we assigned to each title for fund accounting purposes. At the end of the list we added any additional titles that could also be converted from direct subscriptions, as we had been routinely converting these orders when they were up for renewal and available via agent. Our list was ready, then, in time for the year's renewal. Prior to mailing the transfer to our agent, we contacted our other vendors either by phone, or in person — as well as in writing — explaining our decision not to renew and that we were transferring our orders. Careful attention to details by support staff and our service representative allowed the transition to proceed smoothly, enabling us to receive one invoice for all of our titles in time for the next renewal period.

BENEFITS OF CONSOLIDATION

It has been two years since we consolidated our orders and we continue to convert direct orders as they become available. Now nearly 80% of our orders are with one domestic agent and the remainder break out as follows: 5% are direct and the remaining 15% are depository, gift, exchange, or free. We have been pleased with the overall success of our consolidation — with no duplicate subscriptions and few titles falling between the cracks. Our service charge for 1989/90 is less than 5%. Further, we are now using our agent to order back issues, saving us much staff time.

The management reports we have received that list our subscriptions alphabetically by title, sorted by subject and division, broken down by country of origin, or illustrating historical price changes are now more useful, because we have less work to do to enhance this information with direct title data maintained in our in-house database. In the future we will explore having our agent carry these remaining titles as well, allowing us to drop maintenance of the in-house database and attain reports listing all of our titles.

Acquisitions work has been simplified for the staff. We are now able to use the same claim format for our titles. We no longer have to deal with varying forms and requirements of several vendors, and our vendor representatives continue to give us excellent service.

With NOTIS implementation our sales representative provided us with an information report for all of our titles, enabling us to enhance our NOTIS acquisitions database with information regarding claiming, table of contents and index inclusion, and titles received with memberships and subscription packages. In addition, our agent worked closely with us to utilize the invoice tapeload program which we will be using regularly in the future for our supplemental billings and credits. We have successfully loaded this program twice, saving the support staff hours of individual title postings, as we assigned our journals to subject areas for fund accounting.

For our renewal this year we will not need a quote as our confidence is high, due to the number of reports we have received and the online invoice processing we have done. Therefore, for the first time we will be able to take advantage of depositing our money in advance, thereby benefiting from the discount for early renewal. Our success with consolidation can best be summed up by Tuttle:

> consolidation permits the library to process the fewest number of invoices to deal with only one agency. If the vendor's computers compile management data, that information will be more useful than if the orders are divided among several sources, since it will include nearly all of a library's current serial orders.[13]

FUTURE CONSIDERATIONS

The advantages of list consolidation have been enumerated, but the library might review the list using the guidelines established by Doris New for placing orders with agents or with publishers.[14] Were any titles placed with the agent that should have been kept direct in order to receive special discounts? Could the service charge be reduced if very expensive titles were removed and placed with the publisher, especially if a price differential was included? Are delivery services prompt? To date, user demands for newspapers to be available more quickly made it necessary to remove these titles from the list and replaced with a local delivery service. These considerations must, of course, be balanced with the benefits received from consolidation of the subscription lists.

REFERENCES

1. Rutledge, John and Luke Swindler. "The Selection Decision: Defining Criteria and Establishing Priorities," *College and Research Libraries* 48 (March 1987): 123-131.

2. "The Future Revealed," *American Libraries* 20 (February 1989): 108.

3. Magrill, Rose Mary and John Corbin. *Acquisitions Management and Collection Development in Libraries*. 2nd ed. (Chicago: American Library Association, 1989): p. 6.

4. Kuntz, Harry. "Serials Agents: Selection and Evaluation," *Serials Librarian* 2 (Winter 1977): 143-144.

5. Ibid.

6. Derthick, Jan and Barbara B. Moran. "Serial Agent Selection in ARL Libraries," in *Advances in Serials Management* (Greenwich, Connecticut: JAI Press, Inc., 1986): 1:5.

7. Ibid., p. 19-20.

8. Schmidt, Karen A. "Choosing a Serials Vendor," *Serials Librarian* 15 (Winter 1988): 12.

9. Basch, N. Bernard "Buzzy." Determining Which Subscription Agency Services Best Meet Your Needs," *Serials Librarian* 17 (Winter 1990): 82.

10. Sanders, Thomas R. "Subscription Agents in an Automated World," *Serials Librarian* 15 (Winter 1988): 45.

11. New, Doris. "Serials Agency Conversion in an Academic Library," *Serials Librarian* 2 (Spring 1978): 277-285.

12. Anderson, Jan. "Order Consolidation: A Shift to Single Vendor Service," *Serials Librarian* 17 (Winter 1990) 93-97.

13. Tuttle, Marcia. *Introduction to Serials Management* (Greenwich, Connecticut: JAI Press Inc., 1983): p. 81.

14. New, Doris E. "Serials Agency Conversion," p. 277-285.

Awarding Acquisitions Contracts by Bid or the Perils and Rewards of Shopping by Mail

Frank B. Dowd

SUMMARY. This article describes the process of developing bid specifications for sending library materials contracts out to bid so that desirable bids from reliable vendors may be received. It details the things which must be negotiated with any purchasing department including criteria for bid evaluations and contract awards. The article notes problems which may arise in the bid process and sets out ways to deal with these. The need for contract monitoring is described, as is the need to amend contracts from time to time. The article endeavors to set out a method whereby the bid process may work to the advantage, not the disadvantage, of the library.

Purchasing by competitive bid is becoming an issue that more and more acquisitions librarians must deal with. Because of tighter budgets and the need to justify every expenditure, acquisitions librarians frequently no longer have the freedom they once did to purchase from the same established vendors year after year. Increasingly, university, county, or municipal purchasing departments are questioning every purchase and demanding documentation that the library is getting the best buy for its dollar. How the bid process works, and more specifically how it can work to the advantage of the library, is the subject of this article.

Frank B. Dowd is Acquisitions and Special Collections Manager at Montgomery County Department of Public Libraries, 99 Maryland Ave., Rockville, MD 20850.

DEVELOPING BID SPECIFICATIONS

Clear, unambiguous product specifications are the heart and soul of any bid solicitation. In developing bid specifications, the acquisitions librarian will need to be very clear in defining what is to be purchased. The purpose of developing bid specifications is to get control over the process of the bid and define the product in such a way that competitive purchasing may take place. Generally, acquisitions librarians are wary of the process of purchasing through competitive bid, and rightly so. The process is inherently flawed if the product is not carefully defined and safeguards are not employed to screen out vendors who would seek to use the process to the library's disadvantage.

No two vendors are alike. Vendors have different strengths and weaknesses as well as different special services. One vendor may be excellent at supplying current trade fiction at the lowest cost but may not be able to provide non-fiction titles from smaller publishers. Conversely, another vendor may specialize in small press publications but not offer trade fiction at competitive prices. Lumping trade fiction and small-press non-fiction together in the library's bid specifications as one category of "books" deprives the library of bids from specialized vendors and ultimately limits the library's purchasing options. This should be avoided at all costs.

Libraries purchase a whole range of materials today. Books, compact discs, videocassettes, microfilm, and computer software are just some of the things that acquisitions departments now purchase routinely. It is important to take time and care to describe exactly what is being purchased. In the bid solicitation for the books contract, for example, one will want to separate out as many kinds of books as are purchased by the library and bid each as a separate category or separate bid altogether. For example, if the library has always had problems with university press publications, one will want to make this a separate category. Similarly, if the library cannot afford to purchase all society and association publications directly, these should be made a separate category as well, and so on. The bid should be so constructed that bids for each separate category are solicited.

It is not uncommon to have many different bid solicitations, all with several subcategories. In the author's library, for example, the following invitations for bid were sent out. Eventually contracts were negotiated for each subcategory with a total of 25 different vendors.

- *Library books*, with 14 subcategories, including: adult trade with cataloging, processing, and electronic order system; juvenile trade with cataloging, processing, and electronic order system; publisher's trade library editions with electronic order system: reference trade books with electronic order system; best-selling university press books with electronic order system; small press books; large print books; emergency purchases: rebound paperback books with appropriate library bindings; specialized reference books; specialized university press books; society, institute, association, technical, medical or scientific books; domestic standing orders; foreign standing orders.
- *Paperback books*, with three subcategories: children's mass market; young-adult mass market; adult mass market.
- *Foreign language books*, with six subcategories: Chinese; Korean; Vietnamese; Spanish; German; French.
- *Nonprint library media with cataloging and processing services*, with four subcategories: compact discs: phonograph records: audiocassettes; educational videocassettes.
- *Audiovisual media* without cataloging and processing services, with two subcategories: mass-market videotape; and books on tape with suitable library packaging.

Because each subcategory was clearly defined and there were sufficient bids to evaluate (over 50 were received), it was possible to make awards to appropriate vendors in all these subcategories. Having 25 different vendors under contract is of enormous benefit in that it allows the flexibility to place orders where one can get the best buy from the most reliable vendor.

NEGOTIATING CRITERIA FOR CONTRACT AWARDS

The library cannot usually proceed with the bid process on its own. Usually there must be some amount of negotiation between the library and the purchasing department regarding criteria for evaluating bid responses and making contract awards. The purchasing department will be chiefly concerned about lowest cost, but it is critical that the library define the set of minimum acceptable standards which must be met before any consideration of lowest cost can take place. Only the library is qualified to do this.

It is important to impress on the purchasing department the idea that cheapest is not always best if the library's needs remain unmet. Vendors who are in any way unreliable should not be awarded contracts, no matter what they bid. It is also crucial to impress on the purchasing department that the library must be able to verify whether or not the vendor is capable of delivering under the terms and conditions set. If, for example, the vendor is not reliable or has no proven track record in supplying a certain category of material it will not prove to be the lowest cost at all if an award is made and the vendor later defaults. Similarly, if the vendor takes forever to supply, it will do the library no good to have a vendor under contract who cannot deliver in a timely manner. In the same vein, a vendor who does not maintain a sufficient stock of books to supply in large enough quantities will be of no use to the library, even though he or she may have been awarded a contract based on lowest cost.

What are the minimum standards that vendors must meet? What abilities must they demonstrate besides the ability to sell books? Generally, these include a whole range of things which allow purchasing to take place in a reliable, responsible, business-like manner. They may also vary greatly depending on the types of materials purchased. Some common basic vendor qualifications include the following:

- ability to adhere to clearly defined delivery schedules. Tightly defined schedules and fulfillment rates are best.
- reputation and reliability of the vendor. Frequently, it may be necessary to request three letters of reference. This can be ex-

tremely useful in weeding out vendors who bid low but have a poor reputation for delivery.

- ability to provide suitable management reports including back-order status, cancellations, inflation statistics from one year to the next, and an annual report of transactions. One must define the reports that the library must have and include these as a condition of awarding a contract.
- ability to provide selection assistance, including such things as microfiche or CD-ROM stock reports, catalogs, and so forth.
- adequate stock to select from if one desires to purchase in person.
- adequate customer service including toll-free telephone number and a particular assigned customer service representative.
- clear written evidence from the vendor of ability to meet unusual terms and conditions of the bid. If the library is calling for machine-readable cataloging for Chinese language materials, for example, the vendor should be able to produce evidence that this can be supplied.

Once basic minimum standards have been negotiated with the purchasing department and defined, the library may then negotiate how much weight to give to other factors, including those discovered during the bid process itself. Sometimes these negotiations will take place after bids have been received. Some of these factors include the following:

- hard-to-find materials and services such as up-to-date computer books and knowledgeable vendor assistance, or certain small press publications which one may not have listed as a separate category in the bid. One will want to negotiate with purchasing to include these vendors under contract if at all possible.
- prompt payment discount. Sometimes vendors will specify prompt payment discounts. One will want to negotiate how much weight to give to them depending on the library's ability to take advantage of them.
- length of contract. If it is possible to have multiple-year, or

renewable contracts this is frequently preferable. Generally this can be negotiated in advance of the bid.

- ability to amend the contract once it is in place. This can be crucial if the vendor develops new services or if the library's needs change. Prices may change during the course of the contract. Many things can come up and it is desirable to amend a contract rather than have to rebid it.

Frequently, the library will be able to negotiate other, specific conditions for contract awards which are in its own best interests. Two such additional concessions from the purchasing department will help enormously if they can be negotiated. These are as follows:

- ability of the library to make awards to multiple vendors for the same category of materials, in the best interests of the library. If the library can convince the purchasing department that it is in the library's best interests to have a range of vendors to purchase from, provided that all are in the same relative price range, this is much to the advantage of the library.
- ability to award to back-up vendors. One may want to consider a separate bid category just for vendors who will supply materials not delivered by the primary vendor. If this is the case, make certain that delivery specifications are very tight for the primary vendor.

Purchasing departments frequently must be convinced that multiple awards produce the best buy, but it may always be argued that competition among vendors is healthy, and that their knowledge that they do not have exclusive contracts is incentive for doing better.

DEVELOPING QUOTATION FORMS

Once the library has negotiated the criteria and conditions for awarding contracts, one may proceed to develop quotation forms whereby bids may be evaluated. These should be specific and provide room for enough information from the vendor so that bids may be adequately judged. There should be enough space for vendors to describe services which are required, and space for them to attach additional information if that would be helpful.

Frequently, prices may be quoted as a percentage discount off list price. This can be done if there are standard list prices, such as those quoted in *Books in Print* or other sources. Even here, though, one has to pin down what the vendor's actual list price is. Is he or she quoting on a title with freight pass through? Is he or she quoting on the pre-Christmas or post-Christmas price? Sometimes, it is not possible to quote as a percentage off list price. For example, compact discs or certain foreign language materials have no clear list price. For these and other materials, it will be necessary to get quotations on specific titles in order to evaluate who has the lowest price. This may be a tedious process when listing Vietnamese titles or popular compact discs, for example, but there must be a standard instrument by which price quotations may be compared.

Communication is important in order to develop a roster of potential bidders. It is essential to research what vendors are out there and talk to them about the library's upcoming bid. In this way, the library can communicate what it is seeking, and the vendor has the chance to provide feedback to the library about the potential of his or her ability to provide those services and at what cost. There is no point in developing bid specifications in a vacuum if the resulting bid will not get any responses. Frequently, feedback from vendors to a library is essential to the development of a set of realistic and reasonable bid specifications. In addition to talking to vendors at conferences, meeting with vendors' representatives, and soliciting bids from vendors the library normally uses, it is always useful to check with other libraries to determine how they have fared with particular vendors in the past.

Often, it is desirable to have some smaller local vendors under contract. These vendors may provide books which are otherwise hard to get, or they may make all the difference in getting "rush" materials delivered by the next day. With smaller vendors, however, it may be necessary to talk them through the entire bid and convince them that the library will, in fact, do business with them if they are awarded a contract. It is not uncommon for smaller vendors to simply toss the bid in the trash if there is not a follow-up telephone call from the library urging them to bid.

Answering questions from vendors about the bid is an integral part of getting responses to it. It is not ethical, however, to tell vendors what to bid since the process is supposed to be competitive. Nor is it ethical to communicate knowledge of one vendor's bid to another during this process. One must always make sure to check with the purchasing department about any specific regulations regarding communicating with vendors during the bid process. A simple clarifying telephone call to purchasing at the beginning of the process may save major headaches later on.

EVALUATING BID RESPONSES

The question naturally arises as to who evaluates the bid responses, the library or the purchasing department? It is essential that the library play a major role in the process, and at least make award recommendations to purchasing. Ultimately, purchasing would then make the ultimate contract awards to the vendors and take care of the mechanics of getting vendors under contract. The library should do everything it can to retain control of as much of the bid evaluation process as possible.

There must always be a clear statement of criteria used to evaluate bid responses. Frequently, the library will want to state these in the bid document itself so that all who bid know what they are, and also so that there will not be any challenges to the awards. Frequently, multiple awards may be justified if bids are extremely close in price. Sometimes a simple memorandum from the library to the purchasing office stating how decisions were arrived at will suffice. At other times, it may be desirable and necessary to assign points for responses to certain criteria and make the awards on the basis of the highest score.

It is important to take time to evaluate bid responses carefully so that one is clear about the vendors' bids. Often, this can be a time-consuming process as different responses are tallied and evaluated, but it is ultimately time very well spent. This is the time to check references, and determine what evidence there is that vendors are indeed reliable and able to deliver what they have bid. It may be desirable to have a committee evaluate responses so that there is no possibility of playing favorites and no appearance of one person making the choice in a vacuum.

Occasionally, bids will arrive from vendors which either make no sense or which are obviously based on a false set of assumptions. This may be due to a number of things: failure to understand the bid, typographical errors, wrong assumptions about what the library is requiring, and so forth. When this happens, it is essential to consult with the purchasing department as to how to proceed. It may sometimes be possible to talk to the vendor and secure a substitute quotation. The most important thing, frequently, will be the need not to have to send a contract out to bid because of a mistake on the part of a vendor which can easily be rectified. There is a fine distinction between coaching a vendor, however, and seeking clarification of the bid. Under no circumstance does the library wish to be perceived as "helping" one vendor secure a contract over another.

Award recommendations must be clear statements of what the library wishes to do and what the rationale is. If there are specific categories in the bid specifications, the library needs to state clearly which categories it is recommending to award, and which ones it is not. If there are multiple awards to be made, the rationale must be clearly stated and the categories clearly specified. Occasionally, the library may receive different options as part of a vendor's bid. In this case it is important to specify which option the library is choosing and why, and to request that a contract be drawn up expressing one particular option over another.

Contract awards may take some time on the part of the purchasing department. A lengthy review process may be required to determine whether or not the library has made the best decisions. Once award recommendations are agreed to, it may take another two to three months to secure requisite signatures, secure approval that the contract document is legal and not flawed in some basic way, and make sure that the vendor is in compliance with insurance requirements or other requirements such as minority subcontracting beyond a certain dollar amount. This period of time always seems like an eternity to the library but it is essential to plan ahead for a long time lapse between award recommendation and securing a signed contract.

It may be possible, if time is getting very short and one contract is about to lapse before another is secured, for the library to get an emergency extension of its current contract. Generally, this will necessitate planning far enough in advance to take into account the amount of time needed to process an emergency extension. This may also take two months or more so it is important to start early.

CONTRACT MONITORING AND CONTRACT AMENDMENTS

During the life of the contract, it may be necessary to amend it to take into account any number of new factors which did not exist when the contract was first entered into. These may include price increases, new materials (particularly for processing), new services which the library desires, changes in delivery schedules, and so forth. Contract amendments generally require the approval of the purchasing department and frequently must be made in a specific form. The purpose of an amendment, however, is to allow for necessary changes in the working relationship with the vendor and to avoid having to go out for rebid. Contract extensions generally happen automatically, unless the vendor is in default of contract in some way.

Contract monitoring is extremely important if the contract is to work successfully. This entails monitoring discount and delivery time, and also required services of the vendor such as reports, customer service, back-order statements, and so forth. The purpose is to make sure that the library is in fact getting what it bargained for.

The library will need to develop some form of contract monitoring procedures and assign this responsibility to a specific staff member. An automated acquisitions system can aid in providing statistics for various categories of materials so that one can see if the discount bid is the discount given. Spot checking of invoices is another method which can be used well. One may want to develop monthly or quarterly reporting cycles, particularly for new vendors.

When problems arise with the new contract, and they inevitably will, it is important to communicate these problems to the vendor and seek resolution of the problem at hand. Sometimes there may be a simple misunderstanding which can easily be rectified. At other times, however, there may be major problems with a particular vendor which cannot be resolved. In these cases, it is extremely important to have monitored the success of the contract and documented failures on the vendor's part. Contract terminations are much easier to pursue if evidence has been gathered that failures are in fact real and not just apparent.

CONCLUSIONS

Libraries which do not take an active role in defining specifications for the bid process run the risk of losing a lot. Poorly written bid specifications frequently have the result that one vendor gets the contract for everything, and this should be avoided if at all possible. No vendor can supply everything, no matter what he or she may state, so the net result is that the library gets poor service and is ultimately worse off for having gone out to bid in the first place.

One can see, however, that the bid process can work to the advantage of the library if bid specifications are carefully written so that sufficient bids from reliable vendors are received. Ultimately, it is possible to have many different vendors under contract, each for specific services. Bidding can be beneficial to the library but the whole effort demands determination, good communication and negotiating skills, tenacity, and much patience.

Foreign Acquisitions:
Frustration and Fun!

Linda S. Vertrees

SUMMARY. Foreign acquisitions of books and related materials is a series of complex problems, frustrations, accomplishments, and fun. The policies and procedures developed over the last five years by the Chicago Public Library are presented as one library's solution to these problems. Turning these frustrations into successes with the help of public service librarians and vendors is one aspect of the solution. Two different ordering methods: title-by-title purchase orders and profile orders are also discussed; while the advantages and disadvantages of each method are analyzed. Also mentioned is the Library of Congress Overseas Operations Division and how the Chicago Public Library uses this organization to expand its holdings of difficult-to-obtain foreign languages. The acquisitions problem of limited information in general is addressed in a series of suggestions in the conclusion.

INTRODUCTION

Chicago is an ethnically diverse city in which to live and work. With so many different ethnic groups the Chicago Public Library must respond to foreign language requests on many different levels, depending on the situations. The Chicago Public Library is both a public library and one of four Reference and Resource centers for Illinois. Therefore, the Library responds to the requests for popular books as well as scholarly or technical books in 47 foreign languages. This number increases regularly as the Library's collection development goals are modified to reflect the changing ethnic pro-

Linda S. Vertrees is Head of the Acquisitions Division, Chicago Public Library, 1224 W. Van Buren Street, Chicago, IL 60607.

75

file of Chicago. Many of the branch facilities maintain popular fiction and non-fiction collections in the languages of their local community; while the Foreign Language Department responds to both the popular and scholarly needs of all the communities. This diversity requires a very responsive, and in some instances, individualized method of acquiring books.

The acquisitions methods described in this article reflect the policies and procedures that have developed over the past five years at the Chicago Public Library. It is the intention of this article to provide basic information for new acquisitions librarians or librarians who occasionally buy foreign language material. For old hands at foreign acquisitions, this article may be an interesting exercise.

What is meant by *Foreign*? What is meant by *Acquisitions*? What is one person's frustration is another's fun, etc. Before proceeding, common language is needed if this article is to be at all helpful. First, there are basically two types of foreign purchases:

1. Foreign language material (books, phonodiscs, periodicals, etc.) available in the United States.
2. Material purchased outside the United States

   a. Foreign language material
   b. English language material.

What is meant by acquisitions? At the Chicago Public Library collection development and material selection are decentralized. That is, a public service librarian decides what titles to purchase, fills out the order forms and sends the forms and any relevant information to the Acquisitions Division. It is the responsibility of the Acquisitions Division to decide which vendor to use in purchasing the material. Acquisitions is also responsible for the receipt and payment of the books and related materials. (Throughout this article the terms "material" and "book" will be used interchangeably, as the context dictates. The information supplied can be applied to any other type of material ordered.)

ACQUISITIONS PROBLEMS

The problems of foreign orders are basically the same as those confronting any other order, except for language and place of publication. The life of a purchase order or time frame is another aspect of the equation as it relates to books purchased outside the United States, and will be discussed later. The language difference and/or availability represent the "fun" of acquisitions. It requires detective work to locate both the material and a reliable vendor. Sometimes it seems impossible to find the right material with the right vendor at the right time. And, in a nutshell, this is also the "frustration": the constant running into dead ends, the placing of orders with vendors and receiving little if any of the requested material. Additionally, little or no communication from the vendors on the status of your orders also contributes to this frustration.

How do you turn these frustrating problems/situations into fun? A variety of methods will be presented in this article. After all, the greatest fun is the satisfaction of receiving the material ordered in a timely manner and providing the public service librarians with the material they need for reference. That is as good as it gets, as staff in acquisitions divisions do not receive the satisfaction of providing material directly to patrons.

The material selections are made, the order forms are filled out and sent to Acquisitions; now what do you do? You sort the orders by type and evaluate for problems. Now the frustration begins. How do you turn these problems into successes?

LIBRARY STAFF RELATIONSHIPS

First, have a good relationship with the public service staff. Encourage their exploration of new potential suppliers. If they use a catalog for selection, have the catalog or the order information page sent with the order forms. Call the vendor and discuss the library's ordering and payment procedures before placing the first order. This can prevent problems caused by misunderstandings and unfamiliarity with library purchasing practices. The public service librarian cannot, and in many cases does not, understand vendor and invoice problems. Public service librarians' contact with vendors should be limited to informational questions only. As the Acquisitions Librarian, you should be the primary contact for the vendors with the library. Additionally, this introduces you as the person who will solve his problems (delayed payments, etc.). This also gives you the opportunity to understand his needs as a vendor. For example:

Is prepayment required?
Is there a minimum order required?
Does the library need to establish a credit account?

By dealing with the vendor yourself you have the opportunity to establish a good relationship with a new vendor. This is especially important if the vendor happens to be a local dealer.

This leads to the second point: know the vendors. Use the ALA conferences to spend time in the exhibits looking for "foreign" material vendors. Introduce yourself and explain your problems as they relate to foreign acquisitions. Most, if not all, of your problems have probably been posed to the vendor by some other acquisitions librarian looking for answers. Two of the best solutions to your "foreign" acquisitions problems are title-by-title purchase orders and profile orders. Both of these solutions require the assistance of public service librarians.

Vendors or distributors that publish catalogs lend themselves to the title-by-title approach. Although this approach is great for the Roman alphabet languages, what about the Cyrillic alphabet or the Far and Middle Eastern languages? Another method of dealing with title-by-title purchasing of non-Roman alphabet material is to design a special order form. The Chicago Public Library has just developed a non-Roman alphabet order form that permits public service staff to place an order in the vernacular with title numbers and then Acquisitions creates a line on the purchase order reading: "Chinese title number 1," etc., for each title listed. When developing this form one of the first steps was to discuss it with the prospective vendors to make sure they would respond to the instructions regarding invoicing (the invoice is to read "Chinese title number 1," etc.). This form allows for title control, title receipt, and basic fiduciary control. As with a standard purchase order, this non-roman alphabet order form is used primarily for books, but it can be used for any form of material needed.

PROFILE PURCHASING

A well-defined and structured profile is another possible answer to the foreign acquisitions problem. Over the past few years, the Chicago Public Library has used the profile approach with some success for Spanish language books and many of the oriental languages. This was especially important and effective while the library was developing the collections for two new branch facilities: one, predominately Spanish and the other Chinese. A profile provides limited control of titles (by subject, intellectual level, and maximum dollar value), receipt (number of items on the invoice matches the number of items in hand), and total dollar value of the profile. A profile in the hands of a knowledgeable vendor is an excellent way to purchase material, especially for a local vendor that knows your collection policy and has been doing business with you for years. This person knows and understands the peculiarities of your library, and, depending on the sophistication of his computer system he may know what titles your library has purchased in the last few years. A carefully constructed profile may also be the answer when public service librarians have difficulty identifying titles in a given language. In most cases, vendors have a better understanding of the printing practices and availability of books in foreign countries than any library does. Make use of that knowledge of what will be available in the near future from any given country. Developing these vendor relationships can be a very rewarding experience. You will have an ally against the frustrations of purchasing foreign material. The more alliances with vendors you can develop, the lower the frustration level and the more fun you will have, because you will be able to get much of the material requested. One of the drawbacks of getting foreign material is that public service librarians begin to take for granted that their library's acquisitions department can work wonders. They will begin to request more unusual materials and the frustration will begin again, but at a different level. Such is the price of success.

The Library of Congress Overseas Operations Division is another method of receiving material from countries where there is little, if any, bibliographic information available. This is generally handled as an annual prepayment and profile arrangement with the Library of Congress. As material is published it is purchased and forwarded to the library. Periodicals as well as books are available through the Overseas Operations Division. This procedure has provided the Chicago Public Library with many books in the Indian sub-continent's languages and dialects. The Library's participation in this program is currently expanding to include additional books from seven more areas: Brazil, East Africa, Middle East/North Africa, Pakistan, Iran, Thailand, Indonesia, and Melanesia. The Chicago Public Library's 1990 commitment will be approximately $20,000. This is a truly painless way to expand into many difficult-to-obtain foreign languages.

Thus far, this article has dealt with foreign material in general, and most of the suggestions apply to both United States and non-United States vendors. There is, however, one specific problem for non-United States vendors that should be discussed: the length of time it takes for an overseas vendor to respond to a purchase order. The Chicago Public Library's purchase orders have a life of 270 days before they are cancelled by our automated acquisitions system. For some countries, even 9 months is not enough time for a vendor to respond to a purchase order. The Chicago Public Library accepts books and related materials even if the purchase order has cancelled. The Library charges the cost of the material to the current fiscal year's budget. However, time is a very serious problem if the material was ordered against grant (LSCA, etc.) funds. With these funds, you have two problems. One is the simple mechanics of placing the order and receiving the material before the grant expires. The second problem is educating the public service librarians and grant development staff to be very careful with grant funds and non-United States purchases. Your success in resolving the second problem has direct impact on the frustrations caused by the first problem. A carefully constructed profile may not solve the problem completely, but it certainly can make it manageable.

CONCLUSIONS

As you can readily understand, many of the frustrations can be met by careful planning between public service librarians and acquisitions staff. The development of innovative methods of ordering, the judicious use of carefully constructed profiles, and the development of long lasting relationships with vendors can turn frustrations into accomplishments.

One of the ancillary problems for acquisitions of foreign material, actually acquisitions in general, is the limited information and/or instruction available in library schools. One recent publication *Buying Books A How-To-Do-It Manual for Librarians* by Audrey Eaglen (Neal-Schuman Publishers, Inc., New York, 1989) is an excellent practical acquisitions manual. Of special importance is the section entitled: "Selected Annotated Bibliography," as it provides many suggestions for additional reading. Ms. Eaglen's one or two sentence comments are right on the mark.

Most of the tricks of the trade are learned on-the-job, by reading books and articles (the "how I done good" variety), attending meetings and programs at the ALA conferences, and asking for help from other acquisitions librarians. Networking among acquisitions librarians is probably one of the best ways to learn the short cuts needed to turn the frustration into fun.

Academic Libraries
and Firm Order Vendors:
What They Want of Each Other

Richard P. Jasper

SUMMARY. Do academic libraries expect too much of their firm order vendors? To find out, a number of current and former acquisitions librarians were contacted. They provided opinions and insights regarding: What academic libraries want from their firm order vendors, what acquisitions librarians think firm order vendors want from academic libraries, what vendors think academic libraries want, and what the vendors want from academic libraries. Their answers revealed a complex, changing relationship. Both groups raised issues about levels of expectations, costs of new technology, and the direction in which the academic library-firm order vendor relationship appears to be headed. From these issues, the author concludes acquisitions librarians must become more attuned to their own needs, better at communicating these needs to their firm order vendors, more realistic about the costs of meeting these needs, and more aggressive in pursuing standardization of acquisitions processes.

It was an ALA Conference a number of summers ago, New York perhaps. The weather was hot and muggy and, as is sometimes the case, the emotional temperature at the Tuesday morning meeting of

Richard P. Jasper is Head, Acquisitions Department, Emory University General Libraries, Atlanta, GA 30322.

The author would like to express appreciation to the following individuals who contributed their insights, perspectives, and opinions for this article: Dana Alessi, Joe Barker, Barry Fast, John Larraway, Edna Laughrey, Corrie Marsh, Tricia Masson, Bob Mastejulia, Jan Maxwell, Helen Reed, Gary Shirk, Sally Somers, Katina Strauch, and Lorry Zeugner.

the Acquisitions Librarians/Vendors of Library Materials Discussion Group was likewise sweaty and overheated.

The crisis in serials pricing had yet to appear on the horizon and the question of the hour had to do with technology: Which integrated library system would dominate the market? Was widespread electronic transmission of orders around the bend? What would firm order vendors be able to do for academic libraries? Regarding the last question, a firm order vendor responded with words to this effect:

"For years now libraries have asked their firm order vendors for more and more services and we have provided them. With all this new technology, however, we may be reaching a breaking point."

The implication was that firm order vendors were finding new technology expensive — perhaps more expensive than the market would bear. Moreover, there was a not so subtle hint that academic libraries' very high expectations of their firm order vendors were perhaps too high and too unrealistic — especially when it came to costs. The statement provoked a question that is still germane:

Do acquisitions librarians in academic libraries expect too much of their firm order vendors, especially when it comes to technology?

To find out, nine librarians, all current or former heads of acquisitions in medium and large sized academic libraries, and five firm order vendors were contacted for their perspectives, opinions, insights. The following questions were posed:

For the librarians . . .

— What do you really want of your firm order vendors?
— What do you think your firm order vendors want of you?
— How do you think firm order vendors perceive your needs?

For the vendors . . .

— What do you think academic libraries want from you?
— What do you want from academic libraries?

The answers to these questions, discussed in detail below, get at the original question, the one of degree — do acquisitions librarians in academic libraries expect TOO much of their firm order vendors? They also provide a good deal of insight into the nature of the relationship between libraries and firm order vendors — a relationship that is usually amicable, many times ambivalent, and certainly necessary to both sides. As interesting as the answers to these questions were the issues which were raised. These issues centered on the impact technology is having on the likelihood of vendors surviving the coming decade and the price academic libraries will pay as a result.

LIBRARIANS: WHAT DO YOU REALLY WANT?

The acquisitions librarians identified a core of needs which included quickness and precision in fulfilling order requests, accuracy and timeliness in reporting the status of orders, and good, businesslike relationships with their firm order vendors. One acquisitions librarian said it best: "What I want is the right book, fast!"

Aside from the core needs, academic libraries have very individual needs for a variety of services provided by firm order vendors — services, especially as regards technology, that transcend simply supplying the book. In addition, some acquisitions librarians have specific requirements regarding the process by which firm order vendors are selected, as well as the nature of their working relationship with vendors.

All the librarians agreed that "the right book, fast!" constitutes the core of their relationship with firm order vendors, that "the right book, fast!" is the one commonality of need among academic libraries. Academic libraries use firm order vendors because they perceive vendors as providing a very important service, i.e., expeditiously obtaining thousands and sometimes tens of thousands of books from many hundreds and thousands of publishers every year. The basic perception is that it is significantly easier for academic libraries to work with a relative handful of firm order vendors than with the plenitude of publishers whose publications they seek.

A natural corollary of wanting "the right book, fast!" is needing timely, accurate reports from vendors. If the book has not arrived within a reasonable (depending on the type of publication) length of time, where is it? Is it out of stock, out of print, not available in this country, on back order? These reports, the librarians agreed, are essential if they are to make efficient, appropriate decisions regarding how to obtain the book if the vendor cannot provide it.

Implicit in that desire for feedback is an assumption that firm order vendors will, as one librarian said, "think like an acquisitions librarian and ask the second question," namely: If it is not available in hardback, is it available in paperback? If it is not available in the U.S., is there a U.K. edition? Asking these questions and providing accurate reports as to the answers helps determine what additional steps are necessary, or even possible, in obtaining the desired title.

Another common want: A good, businesslike relationship with the vendor, with such ingredients as open, honest communication, appropriate use of time, a knowledgeable sales representative, and a reasonable understanding of the library's abilities and limitations.

With these librarians, the core needs of quick and precise fulfillment, timely and accurate reporting, and a good business relationship are more important than the particular discount a vendor is offering. Their rationale is that a good discount is irrelevant if the vendor cannot provide good service and that they are willing to take a smaller discount from a vendor who can provide better service.

INDIVIDUAL NEEDS FOR SERVICES

Beyond the core needs, academic libraries' needs vis-à-vis their firm order vendors are highly individual. These variegated needs are reflected in the variety of other services which firm order vendors offer, including:

— Electronic transmission of orders
— Tapeloading of order and/or invoice information
— Direct access to vendor's database
— Ability to interface local and vendor systems
— Vendor ability to supply from stock
— Flexibility in providing reports, statements, and invoices
— Ability to provide customized management reports
— Packaging (i.e., binding paperbacks)
— and Cataloging services (cards, slips, tape et al.).

Collection size, level of staffing, and type and extent of library automation were cited as the primary factors in determining which of these services an individual academic library would seek from firm order vendors. The acquisitions librarians strongly emphasized academic libraries' need for firm order vendors to be flexible in providing current automated acquisitions technology. Technology-based needs, they said, are in some ways the least flexible of their special needs. The acquisitions librarian very often does not make the decision regarding which automated system is used and often has little ability to influence system modifications to meet vendor needs. Furthermore, local extra-library institutional requirements may preclude some technological choices; e.g., although the library's system may accommodate tapeloading of invoices, the university's accounts payable office may still require a paper original invoice. In such a case, the library can make little use of the available technology.

Several of the librarians consulted cited a need not directly related to service, one that pertains more to the way in which they make decisions about which firm order vendor to employ. They indicated they want to see a willingness on the part of vendors to "unbundle" the costs of their services. For firm order vendors to "unbundle" costs means that in determining libraries' discount schedules they would also take into consideration the cost of specific services (e.g., electronic ordering, binding paperbacks, customized reports), not just volume of sales and mix of orders. The acquisitions librarians' rationale for wanting vendors to "unbundle" costs is that only by knowing the vendor's component costs can they make informed decisions about which services they want to purchase and the price they are willing to pay for such services.

Other expectations were voiced in negative terms. There are certain things that acquisitions librarians in academic libraries do not want from their firm order vendors:

— Vendor representatives who are not knowledgeable, who do not know what is going on in the home office.
— Vendor representatives who come to visit not to address particular problems or to present new information, but because you are in a pleasant location and they are on their way to a vacation destination.

—Vendor lunches, vendor parties, boxes of chocolates, coffee mugs, pencils, etc.

The last point was the most contentious. The librarians who raised it admitted to disliking cocktail parties in general, to preferring lunch with their friends, not their business colleagues. Other librarians said it was a normal part of doing business, one that made life more pleasant AND a good opportunity for communication with vendors and other librarians—a service, if anything, to the profession. The most troubling aspect of the question: That firm order vendors might think that acquisitions librarians' decisions are influenced by these activities and a concern that some acquisitions librarians ARE thus influenced.

LIBRARIANS: WHAT DO VENDORS WANT OF YOU?

Just as there was substantial agreement as to what they need from their firm order vendors, the acquisitions librarians largely agreed as to what firm order vendors need in return from academic libraries. These needs include:

—A regular volume of orders. The firm order vendor ought to be able to count on a steady level of sales to an individual library.
—A good mix of orders. In any given week, the orders a medium- to large-sized academic library sends out will include titles which are relatively easy to obtain and others that require a good deal of work. Titles from major mainstream publishers are easier to obtain than those from small, obscure publishers or titles from societies, associations, or university programs, who are often difficult for vendors to work with. A good mix will include a range of titles, not just the easy ones or the hard ones.
—No surprises. If the library is unhappy with a vendor's performance or anticipating major changes in order assignment, the vendor should be informed and given an opportunity to make improvements and/or adjustments. Making changes willy-nilly is unfair.
—Good communication. The vendor is in the business of provid-

ing service; unless the library communicates its experience regarding the vendor's performance the vendor cannot effectively monitor and evaluate its effectiveness.

There was a good deal of speculation, however, as to whether and when firm order vendors would be willing to "unbundle" the costs of their services, providing an array of discounts based on the level of service and volume of materials requested by an individual library.

Although quite confident as to what vendors wanted from academic libraries, the acquisitions librarians were much less sure that vendors really knew what academic libraries really need, want, or can provide. Their concern seemed to be rooted in a sense that both the vendors and the librarians are much less knowledgeable about each other's operations than they should be. Librarians, they said, know less about vendors' operations than the vendors think; likewise, vendors know less about the workings of academic libraries than they think they do, even when the vendor is a former acquisitions librarian.

The librarians seemed very concerned about vendor perceptions of decision-making, especially regarding technology in academic libraries. They perceive the vendors as thinking the local acquisitions librarian has more control over the decision-making process than is often the case. Consequently, the vendor does not always appear to understand the academic library's inability or reluctance to utilize an available technology.

Another troubling perception: That vendors really do think they must take acquisitions librarians out to lunch, host elaborate cocktail parties at national and regional conferences, and send boxes of chocolates at Christmas for the librarians to be willing to do business with a particular vendor.

VENDORS: WHAT DO ACADEMIC LIBRARIES WANT OF YOU?

The high degree of consensus among the librarians as to what they needed from their firm order vendors was lacking when firm order vendors were asked to discuss what their clients really wanted. Three of the five vendors agreed that "the right book, fast!" was one common expectation among their academic library customers. They agreed, moreover, that accurate, timely reports were likewise a basic need and that their clients wanted a good business relationship. One of the three added that librarians wanted vendors to be visible, accessible, available, and involved in the profession, an expectation that resulted in lunches, dinners, parties, and a presence at regional and national meetings—a sharp contrast, with a very different rationale, to some of the librarians' perceptions regarding such activities.

Two of the vendors took major exception to "the right book, fast!" premise. One maintained that librarians did in fact want "the right book in the right box," but that "fast!" did not seem to be of concern. If academic librarians were truly concerned about speed of delivery, the vendor maintained, they would take a retail approach to acquisitions, calling a second and a third vendor, or even publishers, if a first call revealed the vendor did not have the title in stock. The vendor maintained that academic librarians have very low expectations regarding turnaround time. The second vendor maintained that academic libraries have no idea as to what they want from firm order vendors because academic libraries have been only marginally successful in quantifying the costs of obtaining and processing monographs. The second vendor's premise is that unless academic libraries have a fully realized notion of the internal costs associated with obtaining and processing a book, they cannot make informed decisions as to which vendor services are appropriate and cost efficient.

All of the vendors agreed that libraries in general have tended to ask more and more from firm order vendors in terms of services, without paying a great deal of attention to the costs. Acquisitions librarians' questions, they said, tend to be couched in terms of "what can you do for me?" instead of "how much will it cost me?"

There was also agreement that beyond the core needs, academic libraries' needs and wants are highly individualized—sometimes so much so that they are unrealistic. One vendor pointed out that his company's 300 largest academic customers utilize 285 different order forms, that the vital order information included on those forms is presented in dozens of different sequences, that an enormous amount of storage space is required to keep the thousands of pieces of paper individual libraries insist on having returned with the books.

This individualization has had a profound impact on firm order vendors' response to new technology, the vendors said. Academic libraries are perceived as wanting a new technology available as much as five years before it will be utilized. Given the highly competitive nature of the firm order business, the vendors must respond affirmatively to any new technology they see as becoming an industry standard; if not, they will be unable to compete. But because libraries' needs are so individualized and so in need of customization, these new technologies have proven to be enormously expensive. Firm order vendors who have not been able to make the necessary capital commitment have gone out of business; the remaining companies have tried to achieve some degree of standardization "through the back door," either by marketing "free" systems that result in many libraries using a single system or by deciding to work exclusively with system (e.g., NOTIS) employed by their largest customers.

VENDORS: WHAT DO YOU WANT FROM ACADEMIC LIBRARIES?

The acquisitions librarians' notions as to what firm order vendors want from academic libraries were very close to the mark. The vendors cited, as did the acquisitions librarians, regular volume, a good mix of orders, no surprises, and clear communication. Beyond those points, the vendors expressed a desire for reasonable expectations and standardization.

Firm order vendors have NOT wanted to "unbundle" their costs, at least not yet. One vendor maintained that it is not possible to effectively apportion different service costs as some acquisitions librarians would like to have done; his position is that the costs are largely fixed and that they cover services which need to be provided, although some libraries may not want them. Another vendor claimed that his company is ready, but the market in general is not. His rationale is that smaller academic libraries, whose discounts are to some degree subsidized by the sales volume of larger libraries, will see no advantage to having discounts based on level of service and volume of sales. Furthermore, he asserted, these costs are already negotiable on a one-to-one basis with the vendor.

CONCLUSION: DO LIBRARIES EXPECT TOO MUCH?

In the area of technology, the answer seems to be one of "Yes, but. . . . " There is little disagreement among acquisitions librarians and firm order vendors that academic libraries' need for technology is very individual, requiring a great deal of customization on the part of vendors. This need for customization has imposed a great strain on vendors' financial resources and has resulted in indirect efforts on the part of vendors to achieve some de facto degree of standardization. Even so, acquisitions librarians point out that they have had very little ability to influence technological requirements at the local institutional level, a situation that firm order vendors often do not recognize.

In other areas, especially regarding vendor selection and the nature of the business relationship, there is less consensus, either among librarians or among librarians and vendors. It is not unreasonable, if you are an acquisitions librarian, to want vendors to "unbundle" the costs of their many services, among which the acquisitions librarian would like to pick and choose; it is not unreasonable, of course, unless you are a vendor who sees these services as intertwined and inseparable.

There is also the question of how the business relationship is perceived. Lunches, dinners, and cocktail parties are seen by some acquisitions librarians as undermining the businesslike nature of the library-vendor relationship; other librarians and vendors see such activity as a necessary and productive aspect of the industry.

Perhaps more important than these answers are the questions they raise:

— What impact have the efforts to respond to new technology had on the firm order vendors? What strategies have firm order vendors employed? What is the likely outcome for libraries?
— Will firm order vendors begin to "unbundle" the cost of their

services and, if so, when? Why have they been reluctant to do so thus far?
— Will the question of "ethics" be resolved?
— What are the implications for academic libraries? What needs to happen?

Regarding technology, the firm order vendors are quite frank in admitting that their industry is in a shakedown phase, not unlike that experienced by the airline and department store industries. Smaller firms either have had to find ways to become larger, so that they could manage the necessary capital investment, or have had to become specialists, finding a niche that no one else can fill. Companies that fail to do either have gone out of business and will continue to do so.

In a relatively stable market, growing larger means increasing one's market share. Both acquisitions librarians and vendors expressed concern that some vendors were employing unrealistic discounts in efforts to win new customers with bigger accounts. They maintain that some vendor discounts have become totally unrealistic, that they require the vendor to trim discounts for already established customers to subsidize new customers, and that the vendors are counting on increased sales volume to offset the smaller profit margins. The librarians' concern is that once the new customers are established, firm order vendors will substantially reduce the discounts or the level of services offered.

The end result, agreed vendors and librarians, is likely to be just a handful of firm order vendors, who will be less flexible in their services and their discounts. Acquisitions librarians said they are already seeing an erosion of choice in systems. They fear being locked out of using a particular vendor because their local system is not supported, or locked into using a particular vendor's system because they do not have an alternative system at the local level.

As for whether firm order vendors will "unbundle" costs, the acquisitions librarians' perception was that the firm order vendors were waiting for one of their number to make the first move. Attaching individual costs to an array of services that are theoretically sold to academic libraries in general as one package is likely only to intensify already stiff competition among firm order vendors.

Finally, the "ethics" question shows no signs of going away. It will remain a nagging question for acquisitions librarians AND firm order vendors so long as it appears that some acquisitions librarians are indeed basing their vendor selection decisions on such activities as lunches, dinners, and cocktail parties.

The answers acquisitions librarians and firm order vendors provided in response to these questions give rise to a number of suggestions acquisitions librarians might consider pursuing in their relationships with firm order vendors. These include:

- Become more aware of the academic library's needs. It is imperative that the acquisitions librarian know what the academic library really needs, how much it will cost to meet those needs, and how much the library can afford to pay.
- Stop thinking it is feasible to ask firm order vendors for more and more without paying more. There is, after all, no such thing as free lunch. Somebody pays the cost, whether it is the requesting library or a neighbor institution across town. Likewise, academic libraries can no longer expect their firm order vendors to bail them out during lean budget times; the vendors themselves are operating nearer the edge.
- As a profession, actively pursue standardization of acquisitions processes, especially in the area of technology. Standardization inevitably will occur, with or without input from academic libraries.
- Clearly communicate realistic expectations to firm order vendors. Apprise them of local circumstances, explain what will and will not work in the local setting, keep them informed as to likes and dislikes, especially regarding the nature of the business relationship.
- Educate vendors and each other. Seek out opportunities to learn more about how the firm order vendor really operates, invite the vendor to learn more about the academic library's acquisitions process.

It is July 1995. New York's weather is, as always for this time of the year, hot and muggy. The 20,000 librarians assembled for the American Library Association's annual conference wilt while waiting for fleets of shuttle buses to take them to the Javits Convention Center. At the Tuesday morning meeting of the Acquisitions Librarians/Vendor of Library Materials Discussion Group, the emotional climate is much the same — sweaty and overheated. The latest technology beckons, promising new abilities but carrying a hefty price tag. The acquisitions librarians want to know: What can firm order vendors do for academic libraries?

A firm order vendor stands and says . . .

Order Consolidation:
One Step in Containing Serials Prices

Jan Anderson

SUMMARY. The acquisitions budgets of many libraries are suffering from the effects of rising serials prices. As libraries are forced to cut the size of their serials collections and cut back on new orders placed, serials vendors are feeling the effects of diminishing business growth. Libraries may gain more favorable service charge rates and better service by consolidating their serials orders with a single vendor or by showing a willingness to switch all their business from one vendor to another. Now may be the optimal time for libraries to gain by reconsidering their present vendor arrangements.

For several years libraries across the country have been feeling the ill effects of rising serials prices on their acquisitions budgets. The search for ways to contain the damage has brought little result beyond simply dropping subscriptions in order to bring down the total price of the serials list. One cost-cutting measure some medium- and large-sized libraries are taking is the consolidation of serials orders with a single vendor, a step which can reduce the overall service charge the library pays.

Recent increases in serials costs have been due to a variety of factors ranging from the strength of the U.S. dollar against foreign currencies to increases in the cost of paper. To complicate the situation further, as prices rise and subscribers are forced to cancel subscriptions, journal publishers frequently must raise the cost to the remaining subscribers. In some cases, publishers have initiated increasingly specialized journals through the process of branching and even "twigging" their journals' scopes and launching new

Jan Anderson is Head of Serials and Current Periodicals, Merrill Library, UMC 3000, Utah State University, Logan, UT 84322-3000.

journals to fill the increasingly specialized demands. With rising journal prices, these same publishers are now often finding their subscribers forced to retrench, to limit their purchases to the original main line journals in their fields. Whatever the causes of the price inflation, libraries with large lists of foreign and/or scientific titles have been especially hard hit by the recent price increases.

Serials vendors, like libraries, are feeling the effects of rising serials costs. Today few libraries have the budgets to add new serials titles on the scale they did just a few years ago. Budget increases are consumed by rising costs. As a result, many libraries are holding the line at a constant number of titles in their collections, often struggling to obtain the funding needed to simply cover the cost of each successive year's price inflation. Libraries less able to find increasing funds have been forced to cancel subscriptions. This means that vendors which are gaining subscriptions are doing so not through the purchase of new titles by existing clients – as was more frequently the case in the past – but through wooing customers away from other vendors or convincing customers with orders split among several vendors to consolidate the orders and give their business to a single company. Under the present economic conditions, these methods of increasing business have become critical to serials vendors. For librarians, too, there can be real benefits to order consolidation.

Utah State University (U.S.U.) undertook such a consolidation, and the benefits have been apparent. U.S.U.'s Merrill Library houses a serials collection of approximately 6,000 current titles, 4,600 of which are paid subscriptions. The cost of these paid titles will total about $940,000 for the 1990 subscription year.

Historically, U.S.U. had split their serials orders among two domestic and one European vendor. The rationales were that (1) a European vendor was best equipped to provide optimum service and pricing on European journals; and (2) maintaining two domestic vendors increased competition between the two and therefore brought the library better service and prices.

While the argument about a European vendor best handling European titles may have had validity in the past, the present situation is that major domestic vendors now have their own company offices worldwide and have become completely competitive in supplying foreign titles.

The second argument — the idea that using multiple vendors brings the library better service — was probably never true. Libraries frequently reason that if they maintain split orders and give any new business to whichever vendor is presently providing the better service, this arrangement will goad each of the vendors into giving the library their best attention. This approach is obviously unsuited in times when the library has no new orders to place at all. Even in better times, the vendor is likely to give the client extra attention for awhile. As soon as it becomes apparent that there is no further significant block of business to be gained from the client, however, attention from the vendor is likely to flag. Splitting orders among vendors will probably bring less than the best service from each of them.

Good business principles dictate that the larger the account, the greater the client's clout with the vendor. Splitting orders among vendors actually dilutes, rather than strengthens, the library's power. The more titles the library places with one vendor, the more titles the vendor stands to lose if the library's expectations and demands are not met. Vendors, after all, are businesses, and libraries are their customers. Along the lines of the old adage, "The customer is always right," it's also true that the larger the customer, the more right they are likely to be.

UTAH STATE CONSOLIDATES

In U.S.U.'s case, the decision to consolidate serials orders was made on purely monetary grounds — issues of service, within reason, aside. Climbing prices combined with constant state funding had devastated the library's serials budget. The library administration was insistent that even the tiniest monetary savings be found, and order consolidation appeared to hold the only possibility of any savings whatsoever.

Clinging to the belief that multiple vendors brought improved service, the Serials Department resisted the idea of order consolidation altogether. To placate the administration, the department conducted a telephone survey of libraries which had consolidated serials orders. They found that five of the six libraries queried had made the change because of service problems with another vendor. In addition, five of the six reported that no noticeable monetary gain had resulted from the change. In spite of these findings, the administration insisted that bids for handling U.S.U.'s entire account be solicited from vendors.

A Request for Proposal (R.F.P.) document was drawn up. It included eighty items and incorporated every requirement and request the Serials Department had. There were requests and inquiries covering prices and service charge rate, the vendor changeover process, titles to be supplied, invoicing services and procedures, claims services and procedures, management reports, automation compatibility, and general vendor data.

Six vendors were invited to consider the university's R.F.P., and three responded with proposals. To the surprise of the Serials Department, it was obvious that a savings of up to 50% of the service charge rate could be realized. Evidently the library had unknowingly struck while the iron was hot, making their inquiries at a time when, due to decreasing numbers of new orders placed, vendors were especially interested in acquiring new orders through consolidation. In addition to improvements in service charge rates, all three proposals offered more than U.S.U. had asked, e.g., free computer-loadable tapes of CONSER records for the library's cataloging use.

When the three submitted proposals had been evaluated, the library concluded that consolidating serials orders would indeed be to the library's advantage. The resulting reapportionment of serials orders brought savings of several kinds.

CONSOLIDATION RESULTS

The first savings was in service charge rate. Before consolidation the two domestic and one European vendor handled 40%, 24%, and 4% of the library's business, respectively, with the remaining 32% ordered directly from publishers. The service charge rate after consolidation was less than half the composite rate of the three vendors before the change was made. As a result, over $17,500 was saved the first year alone. Over the first three years at the new rate, a savings of nearly $60,000 is anticipated – an amount which is small in the face of the total budget, but is certainly significant.

Another major savings has been seen in staff time spent processing invoices, claims, and correspondence. Invoices are received on magnetic tapes for direct loading into the library's automated system, and the consolidation has reduced the number of these tapes by more than half. Correspondence on claims is now done in a single major chunk instead of three. The library deals with a single account executive and a single sales representative. Time savings have been found even in simple activities. For example, it is no longer necessary to look up which vendor handles a particular title before contacting the company for information or assistance with a journal; there's no longer any question which vendor should be contacted.

To the Serials Department's pleasure, an additional result of the R.F.P. process was that the chosen vendor picked up over 500 of the titles the library had been ordering directly from the publishers. The savings in staff time alone, processing these titles, more than makes up for the additional service charge incurred by acquiring them through a vendor.

Statistical management reports and summaries provided by the vendor now cover 80% of the library's paid serials titles – everything except the lingering 20% which must be ordered direct. This is a real advantage compared with the process of manually combining data from the management reports of several different vendors. Evaluation and planning can easily be done on the basis of the most complete information available. The larger vendors can now supply management reports including and sorted by a wide variety of information fields. Order consolidation increased the usefulness of these reports and therefore increased the library's use of them, thereby saving still more staff time and energy.

On top of the monetary and convenience improvements resulting from order consolidation, the library has realized an additional benefit. For the chosen vendor, U.S.U. is now a large account. As a result, the service U.S.U. receives is excellent. The vendor is unusually responsive to the library's problems and needs. It is clear that by consolidating orders, U.S.U. has multiplied its clout. Ironically, the consolidation of orders and standardization of record-keeping with a single company will also make future vendor changes easier if they should become necessary. If service or service charge deteriorates, the vendor is now in a position to lose a much larger block of business than before the consolidation.

Vendors are businesses, and if the library-customer is willing to disrupt the status quo in order to seek improvements, then the library has power to demand the best possible service and price from the vendor.

GOOD BUSINESS

One indicator of the value of U.S.U.'s business to a serials vendor is the fact that the domestic vendor the library left has made a point to keep in contact. They have shown a continuing interest in the library and have made it clear that, should the library become dissatisfied with their competitor's service for any reason, they are still interested in recovering the business.

Consolidation of orders with a single domestic serials vendor has been a good move for Utah State University. In an ironic reversal of roles, the experience has demonstrated the law of supply and demand. If a library can supply the business a vendor desires, the library can demand favorable service charge rates and attentive service in exchange.

The decision to consolidate serials orders was found to be simply a good business move. During this period of climbing prices, a small but significant monetary savings was realized. The additional bonus of savings in staff time and increased use of automated services made the change doubly worthwhile.

For other libraries which are seeking savings in their serials budgets, a change of vendor may be one part of the solution. Whether the library's orders are presently split among several vendors or placed with a single company, the library may benefit from indicating a willingness to make a change in the present situation. Just as libraries are feeling the increase in serials prices, vendors are feeling the resulting decrease in new orders placed. This fact is likely to make serials vendors responsive to library requests for favorable services and rates. The present period of climbing prices may be the optimal time for libraries to benefit from investigating vendor changes.

Centralized Collection Development and Branch Library Acquisitions

Don Lanier

SUMMARY. Collection development is a cardinal responsibility of librarians. In the context of a library system with a main library and one or more branches, responsibility for collection development in many cases is centralized in the main library. In other cases, collection development responsibility rests entirely with the branch staff and primary clientele. Centralized collection development represents one extreme. Collection development autonomy for the site is seen as the other extreme. Responsibility shared by central and site staff is suggested as a more balanced and logical approach. Responsiveness to user needs iş a key criterion of quality for branch library services. The close relationship between branch library staff and primary clientele produces a unique environment, including service expectations unfamiliar to and unacceptable to centralized operations. It is vital that branch librarians be involved if collection development is to be effective.

The acquisition of library materials for branch libraries presents many challenges to the library staff and administration. In part this is because of the environment in which branch libraries always exist. That environment invariably includes a high degree of sensitivity to the needs of the primary clientele — whose needs really account for the reason the branch library exists in the first place. Another significant aspect of branch library environment is the relationship which exists between the branch and other units of the library system. In some respects the branch library can be treated like any other unit in the system. At times, however, the specialized clientele or the mere size of the operation will result in more varied

Don Lanier is Health Sciences Librarian (Site Librarian) and Associate Professor, University of Illinois at Chicago, College of Medicine at Rockford, Rockford, IL 61107.

and complex operational considerations for branch libraries. Added to these organizational issues are the technical, bibliographic, and economic complexities peculiar to the world of publishing and information. It is easy to see how acquisitions for site libraries consists of more than the basic decision to acquire certain materials.

When a library system utilizes centralized collection development and acquisitions, as opposed to having selection and acquisition decisions made at the branch, another environmental dimension is added. Unlike centralized processing for library materials, centralized collection development has a significant impact on the working relationship and communication between site library staff and the primary clientele.

It may be helpful to review the context in which most branch libraries exist. Quite commonly a specific group of users in a particular location has resulted in the establishment of a separate facility and collection. ACRL guidelines provide some general principles regarding management policies for branch libraries. Among the statements most applicable to this discussion are the following:

- The responsibility for the management of all libraries, both main and branch, should rest with the library administration.
- Library services are most effective when all the institution's library resources are considered part of one system with consistent policies for access, accounting, analysis, and the like.
- The branch library staff should report to the main library administration.
- The materials selection policy for each branch should be coordinated with the main library's selection policies.
- In most cases, centralized processing and acquisitions will prove most economical.
- The quality of branch services depends on its responsiveness to user needs.[1]

It should be acknowledged that there are differentiations to be made among branch libraries, departmental libraries, and multi-site or multi-campus libraries. The organizational issues referred to above influence these differentiations. However, two factors are particularly significant to the collection development/acquisitions function for branch libraries. When branch libraries are characterized by both the assignment of professional staff and by a location of considerable distance from the main library, the focus of communication shifts from the main library to the branch. From the standpoints of expertise, practicality, and convenience, branch library users see no benefit in dealing with main library personnel.

Another consideration has been identified by Lawrence and Lorsch when they say, "Organizations engaged in routine activities are said to be most appropriately structured with high levels of centralization and formalization whereas those engaged in nonroutine activities are advised to adopt low centralization and formalization."[2] What transpires at a branch library which is remotely located and requires professional staffing is not likely to be characterized as routine. Low centralization approaches to decision-making and user services are advisable to the extent that this does not disrupt total library system benefits and cooperation.

CENTRALIZATION – A QUESTION OF DEGREE

Among librarians there is widespread support for the centralized administration called for in the ACRL Guidelines for Branch Libraries. Such centralization is not universally found in academic libraries. Law school and medical school libraries often report to the administration of the respective school or department. And, even when such professional school libraries do report to the central library administration, the school administration exerts a powerful influence on library operations and services. Of course, the school represents the branch library's reason for existence, and it would be irresponsible to neglect user needs. However, at times there are a multitude of ways of meeting objectives, not to mention basic differences in management styles, determining priorities, allocating budgets, etc. The potential for conflict between the library administration and the professional school administration is great.

While the potential for conflict is great, there is no reason to believe it is inevitable. It is quite probable that an approach to centralization will be identified which recognizes the unique relationship between the branch library and its primary clientele. Indeed, as Wilfred Ashworth has indicated, it is the first task of management to recognize the nature of the organization and its set of conditions.[3] Ashworth also points out that branch library patrons commonly relate to the branch as if it were autonomous and are dissatisfied whenever reference has to be made to the main library. He advocates "organic control" as opposed to a highly centralized and formalized control because it requires that each person must have freedom to interpret his own work in the light of his own conscience and the good of the organization, rather than according to rigidly predetermined conditions of service and demarcation of duties.[4] The concern raised in regard to collection development and acquisitions may be more related to perceptions, feelings, and communication patterns than to specific central policies. Ashworth feels that organic control allows the flexibility to be responsible to local needs while supporting overall institutional policy.

There are several recurring fears associated with centralization. For example, decisions cannot be made immediately based on local needs. Personal service in response to user needs is diminished. There is a lack of knowledge and interest in site operations and problems on the part of central staff. These perceived disadvantages of highly centralized libraries are the opposite of what are accepted as the strengths of a branch library. In addition, accessibility and a more congenial atmosphere strengthen the relationship between the branch library and the local clientele.[5] However, David House has warned against equating good personal contacts and strong ties at the local level with a higher quality of library service. He notes that users may still value "their" librarian even when the highest quality state-of-the-art service is not provided.[6]

It is not easy to balance the conflicting demands of centralization and responsiveness to the local environment. Centralization can bring with it strictly hierarchical decision-making and bureaucratic numbness. At the other extreme is the potential system chaos of a completely autonomous remote site.

COLLECTION DEVELOPMENT FROM AFAR

While the potential for problems exists in all operational areas, collection development and acquisitions is the one area in which the conflicts between centralized control and local responsiveness are most often evident. This is understandable because the collection has traditionally been seen as the essence of the library and collection development as the heart of librarianship. Librarians and users alike want to play a part in the important task of collection building. Indeed, every librarian has learned the science and art of selecting library materials. And, every user knows what he or she needs. In academic libraries the debate regarding faculty involvement/control in book selection continues. When it comes to branch libraries, the branch librarian is caught in the middle when central policies appear to conflict with local needs. More often than not the branch librarian is in sympathy with the local point of view.

The primary issue is the right to select a particular title as opposed to responsibility for overall collection development policy. Collection development policies are broad statements of intent which have a macro-level result, which in turn may be indiscernible in the short run. Selecting individual titles, on the other hand, represents a micro-level decision where the result is immediately evident. The strictly centralized approach retains control of even the micro-level decisions. A more balanced approach consists of a centrally administered overall policy developed with the participation of branch librarians and users. Decentralized implementation is then handled at the branch library level.

Are there dangers inherent in decentralized responsibility for collection development? It is to be expected that the branch librarian would support overall policy which is logically developed and clearly articulated. It is unlikely that a pattern of selection contrary to policy would occur. And even isolated "out-of-scope" selections might serve a new or spontaneous need not anticipated by formal policy. Robert Seal has provided an excellent summary of "The Centralization – Decentralization Debate" in academic branch libraries.[7] He refers to the interesting observation that most of the literature on the pros and cons of departmental libraries represents only statements of opinion, little in the way of systematic research having been done.

Keeping in mind the differentiation which can be made for departmental, branch, and site libraries, it remains that accessibility is most often the dominant strength of branch or site libraries. Of course, the other advantages and disadvantages come into play as policies and services are developed and implemented. That is, library policy will seek to emphasize the strengths of both centralization and decentralization in collection development and acquisitions policies and procedures.

CONTROL VS. RESPONSIVENESS

There are several specific areas of responsibility in collection development/acquisitions work which can be controversial in light of the centralization and decentralization debate. The right to select an individual title has been mentioned previously. Even in environments with high levels of centralization, branch library staff and users are usually encouraged to submit "recommended purchases." Such requests are typically assigned a high priority. This does not represent the "Give 'Em What They Want" philosophy so much as it is perhaps a recognition of the requestor's expertise about his or her own needs and, perhaps, in the subject area as well. Too, the political liabilities of being unresponsive to expressed user needs are substantial for both the main and branch library. Approval plans and other automatic acquisition procedures are in most cases confirmation that user demands are valid, and the decision-making process can therefore be expedited.

The involvement of branch librarians is central if they are to fulfill their responsibility as professionals in developing and evaluating services and in managing all library operations. Collection development procedures which bypass branch librarians provide efficiency at the expense of effectiveness. Central collection development staff and branch librarians may well agree on collection development policy for the branch. The interpretation of policy, however, does not lend itself to the same measure of agreement. Often, the nature of the branch results in a narrow focus determined by subject and/or user characteristics. The scope of even a very specialized library tends to broaden in the context of a branch library separated by considerable distance from the main library. That remotely situated library becomes "the library" for its users and for all their information needs. Fortunately, electronic access and resource sharing can help bridge the gap between what is held locally as a result of planned collection development and those information sources not collected because they were considered out-of-scope, too expensive, etc. It is essential that branch librarians continuously compare stated collection development policy with expressed information needs.

Gift books and serials can be particularly troublesome to the process of collection development at the branch library. The personal involvement connected with a gift to the branch may not impress main library staff. Gifts may have little or no relationship to official collecting policy. Yet, the close contact between donor and branch staff (in proximity, if not in relationship) warrants a personal response. Branch librarians are in a position to evaluate the nuances which often accompany the donor's generosity. When necessary, the branch librarian also needs to rely on strong central authority and policy to forestall gifts which do not support the purpose of the library. Of course, even those gifts which are not accepted deserve the personal response suggested earlier.

Duplication of book and serial titles is another collection development issue of substantial concern for branch libraries. Of course, most libraries want to control duplication as a way of controlling costs and making funds travel further in the bibliographic universe. The costs associated with duplication have been mentioned in operational cost studies and collection overlap studies. If the branch has a narrow focus, duplication of materials held in the main library may be kept to a minimum – that is, if main does not also have that same focus. More often than not the point of contention is related to the duplication of general reference and popular materials between main and the branch. It is unlikely that a policy on duplication developed specifically for the main library would be fully relevant to the branch situation. Here again, a high level of centralization and formalization may not allow responsiveness to user needs present at the remote site. This ability to respond to user needs is, of course, one indicator of quality service according to the ACRL Guidelines referred to earlier.

Beyond the issue of duplication between main and the branch is the question of on-site duplication. Like main, the branch library will want to exercise good stewardship of financial resources and avoid unnecessary duplication. However, service expectations at the branch may differ from those at the central library because of the critical and unique nature of the work being done by branch library clientele. A general policy on duplication for the library system can supply guidance. The branch librarians will need to be alert to demands unique to the site which justify exception to the usual policy on duplication. Duplicating serials titles for branch libraries presents a real challenge to all those involved. The financial commitment tends to be a continuing obligation which grows at an alarming rate. There is little agreement on the magnitude of costs due to duplication, but the economic climate surrounding serials publishing and pricing requires greater scrutiny.[8] It is tempting for the branch librarian to select a comprehensive array of serials and then blame central administration when these are not all forthcoming. Realistically, in today's world, few libraries (main libraries included) can order all the serials relevant to their users' needs. Resource sharing and document delivery are only partial solutions. Suffice it to say that collection development for serials requires monitoring by both central staff and site staff. Duplication can only be justified when there is confirmation by branch librarians of local needs.

COMPUTER TECHNOLOGY

Computer applications have been present in libraries for a long time, but only recently has technology begun to do more than make some routines more efficient and enhance some services. Lydon Pugh sees "the computer as a focal point around which the library will build its services."[9] Pugh also believes this development provides a great incentive for thinking as a team. It may well be that computer technology, if used properly, can significantly relieve the tensions inherent in the milieu of centralization/decentralization. The strengths of both can be operative in a library environment thoroughly supported by computer capabilities.

Collection development and acquisitions have already benefited greatly from computer applications. Access to bibliographic records, including locations of holdings, is a starting point in collection development. Computerized union catalogs allow a national (if not global) perspective. The same information is available to both central collection development staff and site library staff. The computer can also make the same budget information available to central and site staff and in a timely manner. When branch librarians are fully informed of the budget conditions, it is easier to accept the constraints placed on acquisitions. The provision of all kinds of management information simultaneously to the main library and sites allows all staff to work effectively as a team.

Other areas in which computers are making a real change in collection development include in particular the facilitation of document delivery (e.g., FAX, Docline), the development of full-text databases, and the trend toward enduser/user-friendly interfaces for many bibliographic and information databases. These developments increase the number of ways libraries may provide information for users. Collection development no longer implies a decision to acquire or not to acquire. Central and site staff can work as partners in determining the relative demand for certain information sources and the most appropriate manner of access. Given present economic conditions and the sentiment of the average taxpayer, it is evident that funds normally allocated for the acquisition of books and serials will have to be reallocated if libraries are to fully participate in computer based information services.

The modern library environment offers an exceptional opportunity for librarians with collection development and acquisitions responsibilities. The extremes of centralization and decentralization, if they were ever appropriate, must give way to partnerships in which central and site staff accomplish collection development goals together. Such a balanced approach to collection development in branch libraries will result in greater responsiveness to user needs and greater job satisfaction for branch librarians.

REFERENCES

1. "Guidelines for Branch Libraries in Colleges and Universities," *College & Research Libraries News*, vol. 36 (Oct., 1975) p. 281-283.

2. Lawrence, Paul R. and Lorsch, Jay W. (Statement attributed to Lawrence and Lorsch in a speech – but the source could not be documented.)

3. Ashworth, Wilfred, "The Administration of Diffuse Collections," *Aslib Proceedings*, vol. 24 (May, 1972) p. 274-283.

4. Ashworth, Wilfred, "The Multi-Site Dilemma," *Journal of Librarianship*, vol. 12 (Jan., 1980) p. 1-13.

5. Conyers, Angela, "The Costs of a Multi-Site Library Service," *Aslib Proceedings*, vol. 37 (Oct., 1985) p. 395-403.

6. House, David, "Managing the Multi-Site System," *The Management of Polytechnic Libraries*, (Gower Press, 1985), p. 135-156.

7. Seal, Robert A., "Academic Branch Libraries," *Advances in Librarianship*, vol. 14 (1986), p. 175-209.

8. Conyers, op. cit., p. 400.

9. Pugh, Lydon, "Multi-Site Management: the Computer Contribution in Academic Libraries," *Library Review*, vol. 34 (Autumn, 1985) p. 138-142.

Managing Preorder
Inventory Files Online:
In Pursuit of Integrated Workflows

William E. Jarvis

SUMMARY. The value of online preorder inventory record posting and statistics is stressed. The transition of one academic library's preorder reporting from a wholly manual card counting system, through spreadsheet reporting, to an offline preorder inventory printout capability is outlined. The experience with original "change request" specification and subsequent alpha site testing of the Geac Acquisitions System Active Request Report is described. Routine use of this report at Lehigh Libraries is described, including serials collection development use. Limitations of that current preorder report and desiderata for future generic capabilities are noted, including a brief comparison with some other system options.

The placing of item-selected, preorder searched, request pending inventory online as records in an acquisitions system is a very useful and efficient way to manage preorder inventories. It is also a very system-specific process, poorly understood outside of libraries. Efficiencies can vary due to both local preorder search options and the degree of system integration or type of system in use, although such schemes are, in principle, compatible with a wide variety of selectors' procedures and acquisitions' workflows. Serials request management (and any long term preorder backlog) can be greatly facilitated by the use of such a reporting concept. The development of the Geac Acquisitions Active Request Report, put in general 12.5 release in Spring 1990, is an interesting case of

William E. Jarvis is Head, Acquisitions/Serials, Washington State University Libraries, Pullman, WA 99164-5610.

115

attempting to meet online preorder inventory requirements within an integrated library system's acquisition module. After consideration of the Geac Acquisitions preorder inventory implementation, other aspects of such reporting will be treated.

In 1984 the Order Department at Lehigh University Libraries had a typical manual card file inventory of preorder, pending, waiting-to-be-ordered firm, monographic titles. Initially, the manual reporting of the firm preorder inventory was replaced by a monthly Lotus spreadsheet of search intake, duplicates found, rushes, searched requests on hand, records placed on order over the month, and records remaining which still awaited ordering. The already searched, orders placed, and requests still pending columns were also reported as total dollars and total record numbers. Each departmental fund allocation was labelled in a spreadsheet row. Cell formulae also provided special studies such as by-college and humanities, social-science, and sci-tech division record and dollar totals. Cost average formulae were also used.

The 1986 Geac ACQ request pending inventory control at Lehigh consisted of preorder card files tabulated monthly onto a spreadsheet prior to eventual firm ordering on the old OCLC mainframe Acquisition System. The card files by fund were the preorder "on-hold" inventory. Once ordered, the preorder cards were discarded, since the online OCLC records and offline monthly prints (Fund Commitment Registers) by fund-code were adequate files. In order for a totally online acquisition system to exist, preorder records would have to be listed.

As soon as I began preparing for the Spring 1987 implementation of the Geac ACQ System, it became apparent that something was lacking: an efficient preorder record inventory management capability. Neither by online nor offline print was there an efficient way to inventory (by fund-code or any other means) a *comprehensive* listing of pending requests which would automatically update (i.e., delete request records) when they were ordered. Although Geac ACQ required REQuest record creation prior to ORDer record creation, no comprehensive ergonomical REQuest record report was available.

In addition to the above essential features of a comprehensive, fund-code sortable, automatically deleting title-by-title inventory there were several (merely) *highly desirable* desiderata: online scrolling of preorder record posting by fund-code, dollar and number of records subtotals by fund-code, hierarchical totaling of more than one fund-code, and lastly, a record by status-priority-requestor ID field. Finally, there was a question of what type of sorting the online scrolling or offline printout would have: alpha-by-title, record number, by requestor, etc.

Over FY 88-89 I directed the transfer of all monographic, continuation and subscription orders onto the Geac Acquisition System. REQuest records were entered online, but were not readily inventoried.

The Geac ACQ System (dubbed "Geacq" at Lehigh Libraries) requires the production of a REQuest record prior to the single-command creation of an ORDer record. The REQuest and ORDer records each have distinct numbers, each the standard calendar year two digit and then hyphen, followed by consecutive numbers, i.e., the first REQuest record of calendar year 1988 would read 88-0000001, while the ORDer record would become 8900000023 if it were the 23rd ORDer encumbered in calendar 1989. (Release 12.5 now gives users the option of designating the year prefix digits by FY or calendar year.)

In 1986, the Geac ACQ Release 11.5 had two request record inventory reports. One, the Search Request Report (ABREQ) is of very limited use for calculating the preorder searched inventory backlog. It is not cumulative and does not sort by fund-code. Sorted by requestor name (i.e., data entry person) it has no date range specification and has a very limited use only as an inventory since the last run. It also prints one large printout sheet per REQuest record, hence it is physically as well as conceptually unwieldy! The other REQuest report, the Desiderata Request Summary, APDESR, is much more promising. It is cumulative and sorts by library budget asset account. It lacks two very desirable features; there are no lists of dollar or record totals.

And from the standpoint of workflow efficiency, each REQuest record must be flagged by the data entry of an UPDate STAtus Desiderata field flag to "Y" from default value "N." Then the desired REQuest record will appear on the Desiderata report if a budget asset account fund-code is assigned. Even after ordering, however, the REQuest record still appears on the Desiderata report, until yet another working of the UPD STA screen and change of the Desiderata status field flag back to "N" is done. Approximately two minutes altogether are required to manually reflag this field first to "Y" then to "N." Although not ergonomically satisfying, the Desiderata report was the basis for the improved Active Request Report.

SPECIFICATION AND ALPHA TEST OF THE ACTIVE REQUEST REPORT

The 1990 Release 12.5 Impact Statement describes the new Active Request Report thusly:

> New report (ABACR1) of all active requests entered between specified start and end dates. An "active request" is an unordered, uncancelled request item (BIBR record). The report lists the total number of active requests, and the total amount applied to them, for each account within each agency. To generate the report the batch runs 2 program and APACR2.
> APACR1 CCP's
>   C-Commit against FS accounts (only if FS on order side)?
>
>   A-Select if ANY matching account (Y) or ONLY matching accounts (N)?
> I-Funds % or copies? (Y = %, N = copies)[1]

The Geac ACQ Active Request Report lists a date range, run date, and page number. (Often the report will consist of up to 350 pages.) Then there is a sort out by each Account Number/Name. The five most important column labels left to right are: Requestor (often used to indicate priority or other status), Request Number, Title/Author/Imprint, Number of Copies Requested (this can also be used as a marker by indicating 50 or 88 "pseudo" copies), and Base Price. Finally, the number of requests and base prices are totalled for each fund.

The above described report did not exist in 1986. Its creation was a result of a Lehigh University Libraries' "change request" to Geac, Inc.

Over the winter of 1987-88 "change request" specification language for a new comprehensive, fund-code ranked, offline report was agreed upon in meetings with the Associate Director for Technical Services and the Systems Librarian at Lehigh Libraries. Change request language was agreed upon. The display of a requestor field was suggested along with record totals, dollar totals, and automatic posting of record until ordered.[2]

Lehigh Libraries' alpha site tested this new Geac report capability in June-July 1988. It worked. We have since learned that unpriced REQuest records, however, may not appear on the report unless the systems operator sets a processing flag to that option. (This may be of importance with Serials management printouts.) Its "look-feel" is that of the Desiderata report with two major exceptions. It was not necessary to switch the UPDate STAtus flag to "Yes" before ordering, then back to "No" after ordering, saving operator time. Also, the new Active Request Report listed total dollars and records. The Order Department saved approximately one 7 1/2 hour day per month of a secretary's preorder, already searched card counting. Time was also saved by foregoing the automatic creating or filling out of "request" cards for preorder searching, since the cards were no longer needed to do monthly inventory. We assume that libraries can acquire powerful capabilities from computerized record processing (more efficient processing, better management reports, etc.). But time saving can be a more elusive goal, possibly only when rigorous workflow analysis and managerial reporting criteria are applied. In this instance, time was actually saved by the use of a carefully designed report structure in a preorder workflow.

The transition from preorder card files to exclusive use of the Active Request Report began in July 1988 and was completed in several months. While the report is convenient and a great time-saver for inventorying book requests, its usefulness in collection development serials management is especially striking. The use of status fields to prioritize and reprioritize serials requests pending at (sometimes infrequent) meetings has been a great aid. Printouts can be consulted in conjunction with online records when further data is desired. Serials backfile request inventory has been greatly facilitated, and even non-serial big ticket desiderata can also be listed.

Distinctive fund-codes can be used to isolate big ticket items, or the status field can be employed to indicate "REQ-FOR-BACKFILE." (See Appendix 1.) The status field is a key decision support feature of this report, both as a way to recall previous actions, i.e., "REQ-DEFERRED-ONCE" or to reprioritize an item for possible subsequent selection by collection development librarians, i.e., "PRIORITY-TWO," or "PRIORITY-THREE."

CRITIQUE OF THE GEAC ACTIVE REQUEST REPORT AND THREE OTHER SYSTEMS

The current Geac ACQ reporting format is not only limited to offline prints, it is also an unwieldy printout which has little of the "scanability" and special study by college, etc., features readily available by routine online spreadsheet tabulations. The Geac Active Request Report does subsort by fund-code hierarchy if the library site has specified hyphenated fund-code sections in the preinstallation policy parameter specification stage for the Acquisition module. Lehigh developed a fund-code hierarchy that supported subsorts by HU, SS, or ST division and separate totalling of books, continuations and subscriptions. So at least the humanities, social sciences, and sci-tech divisional record and dollar totals were provided by the Geac Acquisitions Active Request Report and other fund-code reports such as budget and open order printouts.

Geac ACQ also lacks an online access by fund-code to ORDer records. Such a paperless online scrolling capability would be more efficient and ecological, whether for ORDers by fund or REQuests by fund.

Parenthetically, my experience as a collection development manager working to compile cogent, easily scanable book volume counts by classification range parallels my experience with acquisition features of "Geac." Even ASCII formatted dumps of print files performed by the Lehigh Systems Librarian from the Geac Circulation module-driven Bibliographic Reporting System required the use of previously created Lotus spreadsheet templates. The reports available from Geac Acquisition print files are by no means "spreadsheet scanable." Acquisitions managers need concise arrays of summary data, not unwieldy printouts with totals data scattered one row per page. Even if ASCII file spreadsheet import protocols are created by online catalog vendors, why can't dense summary spreadsheet-like arrays be provided directly by automation vendors as part of standard output?

The INNOPAC acquisitions system provides a request pending, not yet encumbered ordered record option, "Status 1." NYP, OP, and big ticket records have been coded on INNOPAC with this preorder record level.[3] Fund-codes can be assigned, making "generic" preorder inventory management of monographic and serial type orders possible. The compiling of a list of a given order type code on INNOPAC is done online as a Boolean operation. Additional subsorts of the review file are possible. Unlike the "Geacq" system's more rigid offline print requirement, the INNOPAC Status 1 order type manipulation happens to be more flexible, permitting a variety of sort options.

The NOTIS system provides its users with the capability to create provisional records in a selection database as an online/reorder inventory solution. One such solution has been devised at the National Geographic Society Library.[4]

This schema is geared to providing selectors with a direct online input and routing of preorder records to acquisitions staff, who retrieve them by searching a locally coded provisional MARC field which is unique to such selector records. Although this single code field entry is used solely to internally route records from selector to acquisitions, etc., in principle it could be used to indicate hierarchy of different departmental funds with only slight changes in coding.

The structure of integrated systems such as Geac, INNOPAC, NOTIS, and WLN can virtually dictate the strategy that acquisition librarians must use to implement preorder inventory control. Geac's Acquisition System works heavily with offline reports, INNOPAC ACQ features online manipulation, and NOTIS usage emphasizes the mobility of a core record through various online updates and upgrades as the record is passed from one library function to another. Hence, it is no surprise that online preorder inventory control in each of these systems takes on the distinctive character of that particular system.

WESTERN LIBRARY NETWORK

Here are three ways that an online preorder inventory might be done on the WLN Acquisitions System.[5] Unfortunately, all three have the same drawback. The establishment of an online record in itself is an inadequate preorder inventory feature. To be really effective a usable title-by-fund list is required, whether online or offline.

The "desiderata" order type is a current option on the WLN Acquisition System. Rather than place an order at the time of order record preparation online, it is possible to tag the input record as a desiderata order type record, and encumber it at some later time.

The on-demand WLN Exceptional Conditions Report lists as report status #1 any "record created more than 30 days ago but not ordered." This reporting feature has several uses, including the review of one inputer's work by an overseer. The deliberate use of this default feature could serve as the source of a comprehensive preorder inventory report.

Since WLN provides no title-by-fund listing for preorders, online nor offline, none of the proposed *ad hoc* uses of WLN to "force" a preorder inventory is of much value, although the preorder preparation aspects of desiderata, exception report status #1 (record created more than 30 days ago but not ordered) and temporary Standing Order template use are typical of the possible "fixes" of an acquisition system. These sorts of approaches should be considered when looking for ways to "force" preorder inventory creation out of an outstanding order oriented acquisition system.

There is a possibility of using the WLN Standing Order template record feature to enter online preorder records that have not yet been ordered or encumbered. The use of online notes fields could inform subsequent preorder searchers that this online record would not be a true standing order template. The standard serials acquisition use of the WLN Standing Order template involves the creation of an in-process order record for each monographic series volume and/or annual renewal subscription order by transferring over data from the STO order record, which itself is never placed in-process or invoiced. Since the STO record is never itself ordered, it is a natural candidate for an *ad hoc* preorder inventory file adaptation.

The temporary use of the pseudo STO option would be a way to "force" a preorder inventory solution from an as-is WLN Acquisition System capability even if no "desiderata" order type or record-not-yet-ordered exception report existed. Acquisitions librarians may find other "jerry-built" prospects in other acquisition systems. The most difficult part of such *ad hoc* attempts may well be the unavailability of title-by-fund reporting.

IDEAL FEATURES FOR PREORDER INVENTORY REPORTING

An ideal set of status fields would be one where numerous statuses could be indicated in parallel columns, with variable sorting by any combinations of columns. Perhaps as many as five distinct status labels would be desirable per each record. Subtotaling of number of records and amount of dollars would also be desirable. Name of actual requestor, inputer, priority, previous deferral of consideration and one or more free text comment fields would greatly facilitate offline printing or even online scrolling review. Alternative sorts, by either alphabetic entry, price or request record-number entry would also be desirable. The Geac ACQ Active Request Report (APACR2) is of course much more limited than this ideal. That report does provide a large measure of "request pending," preorder searched inventory control in an integrated context; i.e., the inventory REQuest records are largely ready for order when the decision to place them on order is made (see Figures 1 and 2). INNOPAC ACQ, as noted above, more closely approaches this ideal.

Going "cardless" with an acquisitions workflow requires not only an online acquisition system but a usable online *preorder* inventory, customarily with a title-list-by-fund reporting capability. There are, of course, a variety of possible search and order file permutations in online acquisitions workflow configurations. In WLN-style (or old OCLC) mainframe acquisition systems for example, a national bibliographic file is consulted for preorder searching and any resultant bibliographic record is used online as the "parent" of the acquisition record. In locally based integrated acquisition modules such as Geac, INNOPAC, and NOTIS the na-

FIGURE 1. Illustration of Geac ACQ monographic request pending list for humanities-journalism. Note use of priority-three and priority-two statuses, which sort together as "pseudo" requestors. (Fund assignment percentage and adjusted price columns to the right are not reproduced here.)

Lehigh University Lib.
ACTIVE REQUEST REPORT   RUN DATE: 11-30-89
From: 05-01-87   To: NO LIMIT

ACCOUNT NUMBER/NAME: B-R-HU-JRN-0000000 /BKS JOURNALISM

REQUESTOR	REQUEST #	TITLE/AUTHOR/IMPRINT	# COPIES REQUESTED	BASE PRICE
PRIORITY-THREE	890012284	COMMUNICATION CAMPAIGNS ABOUT DRUGS: GOVERNMENT SHOEMAKER, PAMELA J. - EDITOR HILLSDALE, NJ: L. ERLBAUM, 1989	1	19.95
PRIORITY-THREE	890012315	FAIR PLAY: CBS, GENERAL WESTMORELAND, AND HOUSE BENJAMIN, BURTON NEW YORK; HARPER & ROW, 1988	1	17.95
PRIORITY-TWO	890012792	RICHARD DURHMAN'S DESTINATION FREEDOM: SCRIPT'S DURHAM, RICHARD NEW YORK: PRAEGER, 1989	1	45.00
PRIORITY-TWO	890012793	KILLING THE MESSENGER: 100 YEARS OF MEDIA CRITI GOLDSTIEN, T. - EDITION NEW YORK: COLUMBIA UNIVERSITY PRESS, 1989	1	37.00

		Total this Pay	# REQUESTS	APPLIED AMT
			4	119.90

tional bibliographic file integration component is not immediately present. To avoid three file preorder search scenarios of paper on-line preorder, national bibliographic, and local acquisitions module sources, the use of an online preorder file integrated into the on order acquisitions system is highly desirable.

In principle, one could use stand-alone acquisition systems with an integrated preorder inventory component. Such a stand-alone file integration of preorder and on order records will not dispense with multifile access requirements due to the separate required access of catalog holdings files. Although "gateway" style access from an integrated system to a national bibliographic utility is an ergonomical convenience, it is not yet a one file, one screen read-out of:

FIGURE 2. Illustration of Geac ACQ serials periodicals request pending list for science & technology-civil engineering. Both priorities were assigned at serials meeting, and sort by priority. (Fund assignment percentage and adjusted price columns to the right are not reproduced here.)

```
                        Lehigh University Lib
                        ACTIVE REQUEST REPORT              RUN DATE:  11-30-89
                      From:  05-01-87   To:  NO LIMIT


ACCOUNT NUMBER/NAME:  S-P-ST-CIE-0000000  /SUBS CIVIL ENGINEERING

REQUESTOR         REQUEST #    TITLE/AUTHOR/IMPRINT                  # COPIES      BASE
                                                                    REQUESTED     PRICE

PRIORITY-FIVE     890004536    COMPOSITE STRUCTURES.  V.10,1989 AND CONTINUE.      1        350.00
                               BARKING, ESSEX, APPLIED SCIENCE PUBLISHERS.

PRIORITY-THREE    890019053    HAZARDOUS WASTE NEWS - 1989 AND CONTINUE           1        365.00
                               SILVER SPRINGS, MD:  BUSINESS PUBLISHERS, INC.,

                                        Total this Pay          # REQUESTS    APPLIED AMT
                                                                    2            715.00
```

national bibliographic utility database(s), local catalog holdings (via national or local databases), preorder, and on-order files. Viewed from the arcane perspective of preorder file inventory requirements, the trend away from one screen national bibliographic utility linked acquisition systems is a step away from online acquisitions workflow file integration. Mainframe-based acquisitions systems like WLN lack only a readily usable preorder inventory record posting and reporting titles-by-fund component to be fully integrated search, preorder, and ordering systems.

In balance, it should be noted, however, that there would always be less than 100% ergonomical one display screen acquisitions workflows, even in ideal national bibliographic utility-based acquisition systems. There will always be some separate paper-online file sources for preorder searchers to consult, at least some of the time. And even if mainframe-based acquisition systems were to prevail against current system market trends, online acquisitions searching on such mainframes would still have to contend with multiple searches of differently cataloged records to find the appropriate holdings record of the searcher's local system. Given such fuzzy edges for even rigidly integrated online acquisition workflows, the less than instant-one screen "gateway" access from local to national bibliographic utilities is an ergonomically acceptable version of a high-efficiency online acquisition workflow.

CONCLUSION

Acquisition managers must take the initiative to set-up preorder inventory management workflows for serial and monographic orders. While differences can exist in system capabilities, there can be preorder inventory opportunities in efficient online design of an acquisition system. Since Geac REQuest record creation is a prerequisite to creating an ORDer record, it led to the creation of an ergonomical preorder inventory report, a "virtue out of necessity" situation. While NOTIS does not require the prerequisite creation of a REQuest type record, the unitary display capability of records for any purpose makes the creation of online preorder inventory records feasible. Regardless of systems used, or institutional item selection practices followed, the adaptation of acquisition modules to provide integrated preorder inventory control would be a useful adaptation. The benefits of serials preorder control for serials collection development decisions are especially high. Also the distinctive system characteristics of Geac, INNOVACQ, NOTIS, and WLN heavily determine the shape of acquisitions modules and hence preorder inventory methods in each. Therefore, it behooves acquisitions librarians to influence the general design of future integrated systems as a whole, and not merely certain acquisitions subsystem features, because the acquisition module specifics are aspects of their general system characteristics. The absolutely integrated one screen display acquisitions workflow can be approached as a limit, but only approximately achieved due to external database search requirements. We can, however, maximize integration of preorder and in-process order workflows online.

REFERENCES

1. *Acquisition Release 12.5 Impact Statement,* Geac, Inc., March 2, 1989. Section 3, "New Offline Features," F2518, p.13.
2. Susan Cady, ADTS and Joe Lucia, Systems Librarian, both of Lehigh University Libraries, worked closely with me in the preparation of the official change request to Geac, Inc. Alpha site data testing operations and subsequent routine report generation were run by Joe Lucia.
3. Stephen Bosch, "In-Process Control of Order Requests for 'Out of Print' and 'Not Yet Published' Materials Using the INNOVACQ Acquisition System," *The Acquisitions Librarian* Number 1 1989, pp. 131-141; This "Automated Acquisitions" issue contains many articles detailing the intricacies of matching outstanding order workflows to systems.
4. Personal Communications, David Beverage, National Geographic Society Library, Washington, D.C., 1989-90.
5. In-house conversations with Terry Buckles, Programmer at Washington State University Computing Center, June, 1990. As an old WLN hand, as well as a library-wise programmer, he immediately responded to my preorder inventory query with a sketch of the STO usage as well as the "desiderata" order type options. This experience underscores the value of dialogue with in-house programming staff in creatively "stretching the envelope" of existing acquisitions (or other) system features.

APPENDIX 1

Status Field Designations Using GEAC "Requestor" Fields in Use at Lehigh University Libraries, 1990

PRIORITY-ONE	REQ-CAT-FOR-REF	REQ-DENIED
PRIORITY-TWO	REQ-NOT-YET-PUBLISHED	REQ-DEFERRED-ONCE
PRIORITY-THREE	REQ-FOR-APPROVAL-BNA	REQ-DEFERRED-TWICE
PRIORITY-FOUR	REQ-FOR-APPROVAL-B&T	
PRIORITY-FIVE		

Above are pseudo requestor "name" options. One of each is assigned to each pending request and are entered onto the inventory records by filling in the requestor fields.

The third column options are used for serials use only: it is possible to keep an online transaction log of such serial collection development decisions, in addition to assigning the above priority, provenance, or miscellaneous statuses. Eventually, it is possible, even desirable, to cancel "REQ-DENIED" status REQuests, although their retention on a report for a year or more may provide an institutional memory of item-selections-denied activity for various departmental funds.

APPROVAL PLANS AND VENDORS

Approval Acquisitions
and Vendor Relations:
An Overview

Mary J. Bostic

SUMMARY. During the past several years the utilization of acquisitions plans—specifically, approval plans—as well as their selection and management has been given much attention. Research information enables a library to decide whether an approval plan is viable as a collection development tool or to assist in its acquisitions program, and to define vendor relations to approval acquisitions. Additionally, the literature is useful to the library which already uses an approval plan but which wants to review those programs offered by other vendors. The purpose of this article is to serve as an overview of the literature in terms of approval acquisitions and vendor relations.

Mass purchasing in place of purchasing books title-by-title is not a new feature of library operations. One dimension in mass purchasing is approval acquisitions. In approval plan programs, dealers

Mary J. Bostic is Acquisitions Librarian and Associate Professor at the Long Island University Library, Brooklyn Campus, 1 University Plaza, Brooklyn, NY 11201.

129

or publishers select materials for libraries based upon analyses of the needs of each library and allow the privilege of approving or rejecting items sent or proposed to be sent on these plans. As most blanket orders and gathering plans also include return privileges, the names of the plans are used interchangeably. The librarian must discover the exact meaning of an offer from a vendor.

Many publishers offer approval plans for some or all of their publications. A typical plan from a major publisher will offer several dozen subject categories for approval acquisitions. Plans often take the form of submitting lists to libraries for selection rather than sending books. These publisher plans usually offer greater discounts than can be had from item-by-item direct ordering and better discounts than can be obtained from a wholesaler. They also offer the advantage of receipt of the books in the library by publication date. Many of the publishers send Library of Congress catalog cards with the books. When a publisher's approval plan corresponds to the needs of a library, it provides excellent opportunities for advantageous purchasing.

REVIEW OF THE LITERATURE

The literature points to the 1960's as the time when a new form of blanket order, usually called an approval or gathering plan came into prominence, and it appears now to be a permanent and valued part of the acquisitions process, especially for academic and research libraries.

It seems to have taken until the early 1970's for the important distinction between a blanket plan and an approval plan to be codified in the literature. The blanket plan refers to an arrangement with a vendor or publisher to supply everything current (or most everything within certain limits) and sometimes retrospective on a particular subject with the library usually not having return privileges for materials it subsequently does not want to keep. The approval plan, however, supplies current imprints according to a pre-determined "profile" that the library negotiates with a vendor or publisher based upon the library's specific needs. In academic libraries the profile would have its origin in the library's collection development policies and guidelines or, if no such documents existed, it would be defined by the college or university's various curricular needs as outlined in a current course catalog. So in a very real sense the development of an approval plan profile helps to focus the library's attention, perhaps as never before so sharply, on its informational support mission within its parent institution. Unlike the blanket order plan, the approval plan would allow return for credit of material deemed unsuitable.

Approval plans have been both scorned and praised by librarians. That the issue was one of great importance to librarians of the 1960's and 1970's is sufficiently evident in the proceedings of four major international conferences organized and specifically devoted to approval plans held in 1968,[1] 1969,[2] 1971,[3] and 1979.[4]

One of the first controversies has to do with the fundamental issue of who was to be ultimately responsible for selecting books for the libraries. Was it to be the librarians and faculty members who understood the needs of their institutions or was it to be the commercial vendors who were said to have no real understanding of the teaching or instructional support mission of the university and whose only interest was in selling books? Other controversy was situated more in the realm of practicality. Proponents of approval plans cited the speed and efficiency with which the plans were able to bring in needed material as opposed to traditional and costly title-by-title selection and organization methods. The fact that making a judgement about a book with it in hand was considered to be a far superior method than selecting from trade bibliographies, publisher's information, or reviews in journals was another point cited by proponents of approval plans.

Opponents put forth exactly the opposite points of view. In their opinion, approval plans *might* bring in material that is needed, although some would heartily disagree from the philosophical point of view described earlier, but the concern was for the material that the plans did *not* seem to be able to provide. Opponents also put into question the cost savings that might result from discontinuing the clerical routines of typing and sending out purchase orders to vendors and publishers. They argued that any savings obtained would probably be offset by the internal bibliographic control and display for selection procedures necessary for the proper functioning of the plans.[5,6,7]

Despite some of the very real problems associated with approval plans, especially with those that started operation in the late 1960's and early 1970's, opinion has been generally positive over the years. This may be due in part to the fact that through the 1970's and into the 1980's libraries have sought to undertake quantitative studies to evaluate their plans so that a successful study gave rise to vindication of the approval plan concept.[8,9,10,11]

The popularity of approval plans has not been affected by the fluctuations in funding for library acquisitions during this period. When budgets were low, the library had to be more vigilant in acquiring materials that adhered rigidly to the current curricular needs as defined in the profile. In fact, under these circumstances the profile would have had to be fine-tuned in order to assure high precision in selection. On the other hand, when budgets were high, the approval plan was able to bring in early and efficiently most of the current imprints in more subjects.

The literature consistently emphasized that the most important aspect of an approval plan is the profile. No library can maintain a successful plan without an adequate profile that reflects its current information needs and is continuously open to modification as budgetary or curricular changes dictate. A heavy initial investment of time is required in pre-planning that leads to the development of the profile with the guidance of the approval vendor representative and after the plan is operational for several months it is often necessary to adjust the profile. It is not surprising, therefore, that the approval plan concept became in the late 1970's and early 1980's a tool of collection management and development rather than simply one of acquisitions.

No single experience with library approval plans provides the definitive evaluation of this acquisitions technique. The evidence seems to support the general statement that an approval plan has the best chance of success when there exists an understanding of the dynamics of approval buying on the part of both librarians and faculty, when there is sufficient pre- and post-implementation planning and coordination, and when there exists a positive and mutually supportive relationship between the approval plan representative and the library. Perhaps the key is the human factor.

IMPACT OF APPROVAL ACQUISITIONS ON LIBRARIES

Approval plans have created advantages in acquisition options for libraries. One specific option is the use of vendor approval plan services in retrospective collection development and in collection analysis. Such a plan will allow the library to strengthen existing collections, support areas representing new curriculum, and provide a means of collection assessment and evaluation in subject areas.

Although the introduction of approval plans in libraries is not a recent development, they have significantly affected collection development practices in libraries. These practices have now been enhanced by recent computer applications. Automated subject profiling, for example, has boosted the efficiency of acquisitions programs in libraries of all sizes by allowing systems to interface easily with one another and by eliminating unnecessary tasks in the operation of approval plans. The computer has also opened up possibilities for enhancing retrospective book buying.

While approval plans have evolved into fairly sophisticated instruments in the past decade, these earlier writings remain useful. The more recent writings report extensively on library experiences with approval plans/approval plan vendors and are significant contributions to the literature.

Reidelbach and Shirk did a series of three lengthy articles on selecting a vendor.[12] Schmidt read a paper at the 1986 ACRL Baltimore Conference which provided a brief current overview of types of plans available to academic libraries.[13] McCullough, Pickett and Posey gave a lengthy discussion of approval plans in their *Approval Plans and Academic Libraries*, (1977).[14]

Sul H. Lee reported on a national conference held in 1987 on acquisitions processes, material costs and library budgeting. Inasmuch as the demands on librarians to find better management strategies and to develop more effective material acquisition processes have created an environment in which librarians and book vendors are examining their methods by which collections are developed, the conference papers present some of the recent studies and ideas about acquisition processes and the management of material costs.[15]

R. Charles Wittenberg, in his article, "The Approval Plan: An

Idea Whose Time Has Gone? And Come Again?'' states that the approval plan concept has expanded and diversified steadily since its relatively recent creation.[16] He sees four current trends that have come to the fore: (1) new approval plans are being created in smaller libraries — libraries once thought too small to be beneficiaries. If an approval plan can become operational in the small library, the library can have additional control over the core collection — as opposed to faculty dominance where faculty-dominated book selection and faculty control of allocated materials funds exists; (2) acquisitions practices, approval plans prominently among them, are becoming automation-driven. In large and small libraries, the vendor role is increasingly shaped by the need to interface with library systems, and by the more generalized demand for machine-readable record services; (3) the issue of serials and the exorbitant increases in the size and cost of serials invoices. The "book budget" is massively under attack from the inflation in the number and cost of journals; (4) there seems to be a trend toward approval plans failing to keep pace with the growth of scholarly book publishing. Wittenberg took a sample of the status of a group of large plans which suggests that perhaps two in five have kept up with publishing growth and inflation; while three have shrunk considerably in their ability to keep pace.[17]

According to Peter B. Kaatrude, in his article "Approval Plan Versus Conventional Selection: Determining the Overlap," the Management Library of the University of California at Los Angeles conducted an intensive approval plan study primarily as a diagnostic check of the functioning of the library's two-year-old approval plan program. In light of the findings of his study, collecting activity in general improves as a consequence of the use of a well-constructed approval plan. The UCLA Management Library agreed that the approval plan system generally saves staff time, realizes processing efficiencies, furthers collection development activities, and broadens selection coverage.[18]

His study underscores the importance and need of a timely approval plan study.

During the 1960's, when many research library book budgets grew rapidly, book vendors and jobbers began to offer approval plans as a way to collect material quickly without placing orders for individual titles. The reasons for using approval plans have changed somewhat over the past several years, however, and today a number of factors, including budgets, automation, and new staffing patterns are causing large academic libraries to re-examine their selection strategies and processes.

Based on library responses to a November 1981 SPEC Survey, the most frequently cited reasons for using approval plans are to broaden selection coverage, save staff time, improve collection development, and realize processing efficiencies.

The most commonly cited disadvantages of approval plans are that they are unreliable or unpredictable; that there is a tendency to accept marginal material because returns involve significant staff effort, and that it takes time and effort to monitor approval plans.

Additional problems include slow delivery, duplication of material, difficulty in claiming, overspending and loss of control of budget, gaps in coverage, less control in selection, and the tendency to rely too much on plan receipts.[19]

The SPEC Kit on *Approval Plans* (#141, February 1988) is based on a June 1987 survey which covered the points of continuity and consensus in approval plan use over the past four years, as well as the diversity of ways in which librarians assess these plans. The 1987 survey also explored the impact of automation and the recent increases in materials costs. The survey contains tabulated survey results; two examples of questions and criteria for evaluating vendors; five examples of profiles, descriptions, and guidelines; three examples of processing and review of approval receipts; and a selected reading list.[20]

One of the most serious current problems for approval plans is the recent and rapid increase in the cost of library materials, notably as a result of dollar devaluation. Concern about this problem is widespread and is having an impact on approval plans. Of 88 respondents, 56 report that they will be reevaluating their use and management of approval plans for financial reasons. It appears from respondents' comments that this concern is not resulting in any reconsideration of the value of approval plans as such. Indeed, some libraries cite financial austerity as increasing the need for approval plans. However, there is a definite trend toward reduction in foreign purchasing.[21]

A second development which has great potential to affect approval plans is automation. It is clear, however, that the effect of automation on approval plans is not yet very great. It seems likely that in the immediate future the greatest changes in approval plans will be driven by automation, as acquisitions systems become increasingly prevalent and sophisticated, and as vendors and libraries discover ways of using this new capability to mutual advantage.

VENDOR RELATIONS

The matter of vendors' service is indeed variable. A library's relationship to a vendor depends on the library's own requirements and is partly the library's responsibility. It must call the vendor's attention to lapses. On the other hand, the library must make an attempt to understand the vendor's position. The vendor, who is responsible for a profit-making enterprise, must keep services to libraries within reasonable fiscal bounds. He is a middle man. He stands between the complexities of publishing and the complexities of academic library service. He also must mediate attempts to standardize the individual practices and demands of thousands of libraries, at the same time allowing as much latitude for individual preferences as possible.

In collection development, the vendor's role in screening and preselecting is a matter of concern. The quality of the collection to which the approval plan contributes, however, is controlled by the library staff and the extent to which it reviews and selects books and the attention it gives to adjusting the profile as the milieu changes. Standards fluctuate, and research interests change. The attitude toward a plan, as in any other situation, is a matter of weighing advantages and disadvantages in the local setting.

Approval plans do work and can be successful. To be successful, they must be as inclusive as you can set them up. The librarian, or the library, is always the final judge of what is to be kept. If the library puts too many restrictions on the vendor, he doesn't have enough room to move around.

The general tone of the literature is that approval plans are for libraries with an ample budget; that the plans must be as inclusive as possible, and that too much exclusivity makes the plans difficult to manage and monitor; that invoicing should be by individual title; and that the beginning of any such approval plan program should take into consideration imprint date — that is, the plan should begin with imprints of a particular year.

The dealer and the librarian have to address themselves to the problem of perception and communication, in order to make precise the specific wants of libraries and what the dealer thinks the library wants. Sometimes, it's probably not quite clear to the library itself what it wants.

An increasing number of domestic and foreign dealers are now offering approval plans to their customers. The great interest on the dealers' part may possibly result in attractive services designed to serve libraries at the small college and community college level. This means the professional book dealers would not overlook libraries in the $50,000 to $150,000 book budget category.

Obviously, there is a great need for a close working relationship between approval-plan vendor and library, as an approval plan cannot be construed as simply a technique used within the library and, therefore, of little or no use concern outside the profession. Although the concept was designed to meet the library's needs, it was the library book supplier, wholesaler or publisher, who executed the design and who must be considered the active, if junior partner if it is to be successfully implemented and managed within the library.[22]

Approval plans work to the advantage and satisfaction of many libraries. Unrealistic expectations from approval plans are frequently the primary source of disillusionment on the part of the library. The vendor must bear his full share of responsibility for this state of affairs. If the emphasis is on efficiency in acquisitions, the vendor will normally emphasize the aspects of his plan that tie in to this expectation. On the other hand if the library indicates its primary interest is balanced collection development the vendor may stress the credentials of his selection staff, the number and quality of subject and nonsubject descriptors, and the staff's ability to seek out and bibliographically describe books in very nearly all known fields.[23]

When the plan has to be integrated within the everyday interaction among subject specialist, departmental librarian, faculty user, and others with differing needs and problems, any lack of basic consensus on what the reasonable expectations should be and what should be the proper division of responsibility between vendor and user will soon make itself known to the dismay of the acquisitions staff and the vendor.

Economics can be documented only in terms of the library user's individual experience based upon hard statistics as these exist within his own library.

Obviously coverage will be inadequate if the profile is ill-constructed. The profile is the heart and brains of an approval plan and is an infinitely complex mechanism.

Both the library and vendor lose as the result of a fundamental misunderstanding as to each other's primary role and responsibility. Profile preparation determines the future satisfaction of collection development requirements. It must be recognized that this is a joint and equal responsibility on the part of the user as well as the vendor. Selection starts with the profile.

The librarian should state at the onset what his budget maximum will be for the approval plan. This way the vendor knows the outer dollar limits and can help if the librarian with a modest budget is prepared to be realistic in his expectations. An approval plan that is well constructed and operated can be tailored to limited funding. It is time that the impression that limited or shrinking budgets negate the advantages be reevaluated.

Therefore, librarians charged with approval-plan-vendor selection need to include or, at the very least, keep informed those who are responsible for selecting and developing book collections. Inclusion of faculty representatives, subject bibliographers, public or reader service librarians, departmental librarians, collection-development staff, or any other constituency, regardless of title but have responsibility for book selection and collection development, is essential.

If a plan is to receive maximum opportunity for its successful translation into a workable, integrated program, then not only acquisitions and administration must be directly involved from the beginning. Communication is the single most important factor within the library as well as between the vendor and the library in successfully implementing an approval plan. According to Pickett, lack of communication and adequate understanding of the concept, is a common thread in most approval-plan failures. No other service maintained by a book vendor has so many built-in features that require and almost demand a close working involvement between the librarian and the vendor as does an approval plan.

SOME CONSIDERATIONS

If the library's chief concern rests with the means of improving the order and receiving processes, consideration of approval acquisitions is feasible, in that it will enable the library to obtain books more rapidly, allow for examination of books received, reduce clerical and professional time and strengthen the library holdings in all fields of the curricula of the university.

In scanning the library literature to see what can be learned from the experiences of other libraries, it will be noted that many studies deal with the wealthy libraries of the nation. They are not typical enough to present to the officials of a financially-poor state a good example. The wealthier the library, the broader the approval plan. It is possible to set up an approval plan with a limited budget if a library chooses to set up its requirements within specific profiles of materials offered by the book jobber.

The library will want to consider enrollment figures — graduate and undergraduate; budgets for books and serials; what effect the approval plan would have on library using departmental allocations (compatibility of the approval plan with their system of budgeting); what percentage of the total budget is needed for an approval plan; will the library require partial approval plan for specific subjects; what about language limitations (limited to the English language?); will the approval plan bring the library most of the items that would have been ordered under normal procedures; promptness of receipt of the book after publication; what services are available in acquiring serials under this system; what about duplicates (if not ordered from the approval dealer, how will additional copies be acquired); bibliographic aids (since most items received are new publications, much time and money can be saved if personnel will not need to check the bibliographic references); what contribution the approval plan makes to the acquisitions process; preparation of profiles to eliminate unwanted material; are there savings in the use of the approval plan program (time saved in clerical work of typing and in bibliographic checking; professional time saved since the system does not require extensive checking in brochures, reviews, and bibliographies; saving evidenced in invoicing procedures and handling of the manifold order forms; printing cost for order forms); selection and rejection of the materials received on approval (libraries aided extensively by the faculty?); selection office staffed by a professional librarian aided by faculty representation?; percentage of returns (keeping/not keeping records of rejections of books received on approval); follow-up on titles the library feels have not been included in the plan under its profile arrangement.

This systematic coverage of a field or fields wanted by a given library can be an asset, provided the library staff is able to define the needed coverage in subjects and level of interest. This by no means implies the acceptance of all works published. Books purchased in this fashion are available before the user wants them, not several months later.

The library staff can do a better job in book selection. A book in hand can be more effectively evaluated than by the use of annotated selection guides, or even full reviews—which fall short of the "book in hand" experience. In other words, successful approval plans are not "automatic" but are based on individual selection policies established by libraries such as subject, quality, level of use, language and other definitions prepared by the respective library staffs.

Because of work simplification, the library staff may find more time for seeking out needed O.P. material. Additionally, libraries using approval plans may realize significant savings in actual operating costs in the library, in faculty time, and in the business office and budget control operations.

To wait for a faculty member or a staff member to order a current title is a little too indefinite. With a full approval plan, the library receives most of the good books. By the time the reviews and criticisms have appeared, the book has been on the market for some time. If it has been on the market for some time, why shouldn't it be in the library for some time?

A host of local conditions and factors must be considered in addition. It seems to me that every librarian concerned with acquisitions should reflect on whether or not an approval plan is applicable and desirable for his operation. Business machines of all kinds have been adapted; multiple forms, automation of various kinds, all have helped the acquisitions librarian keep abreast of increasing demands on his services. An approval plan should be considered for the same reasons these have been, because it can potentially yield the same kind of advantage.

The transition from a traditional way of ordering books to approval order plans involves matters of bibliographical responsibility and fiscal concerns. The plan must be tailored to the institution both bibliographically and fiscally. Close planning is necessary and there must be a compromise in some existing arrangements and routines. Although no librarian should give up his function in book selection, there comes a point in time when the approval order plan may become desirable.

Full contact with the faculty is recommended in putting a plan into effect, as well as a means of evaluation of the plan after it has been put into effect.

Libraries must recognize that an approval plan may fall outside routine procedures and may thus require a separate unit to manage it.

It is the responsibility of the acquisitions department to organize the plan; to construct the profile — in consultation with the collection-development staff, it is hoped; to understand the restrictions of the profile and weed profile exclusions from the shipments; to check on apparently overdue books; to decide whether to claim from the approval vendor or place a firm order; to return all books not wanted for the library, clearing the billing records in the process; to initiate adjustments to the profile; and to maintain separate budget controls.

Some added duties are routine and some are engendered by the political situation that results from the increased interaction between the public- and technical-services staffs. Inevitably, some important books will be missed in the vendor's dragnet, and inevitably there will be some that will be delayed by action (or inaction) of either the publisher or the vendor.

Most libraries fund the approval plan separately. If the approval plan is for a single copy, as most plans are, either interim receipt records must be maintained to direct other requests for the approval book or the source of the cataloged copy must be traced for every subsequent request for the same title.

There is also the complication of whether to order a book or to wait for the approval copy because it is not always apparent from a title or other bibliographic information whether the book is eligible for the approval plan.

A change in vendor may become necessary. Such a change is traumatic for everyone concerned: book-selection personnel, the acquisitions staff and the new vendor. Book selectors suffer through an interruption in service and a waiting period until the new plan is in full operation. Books are delayed or missed altogether. The new vendor's procedures and forms are slightly different, so that there is confusion until book selectors become comfortable with a new set of routines and concepts.

Acquisitions is the point at which an approval-plan procedure starts; collection development is the point at which it ends. It is possible, given staff and time, to organize the special procedures needed for an approval plan into a reasonably efficient routine, at least those that are under control of the acquisitions department.[24]

CONCLUSION

Review of the literature provides a wide range of writings on approval acquisitions and vendor relations, the overall tone being favorable.

A general observation is that approval plans are big business and are subjects of great importance in academic libraries. A great number of academic libraries have had practical limited approval plans for a good many years.

Approval plans have many new concepts and associations, and there are a number of academic libraries with modest book budgets operating one or more approval plans.

Since the major problem connected with approval plans is financial, vendors view with concern libraries' commitment of more and more of their funds for approval acquisitions. However, current budget strains on college and university libraries require a stepped-up search for operating economics; and although approval plans will continue to be somewhat controversial as a collection develop- ment tool, the practice is here to stay and is gaining momentum.

Particular emphasis is placed on the need for a good collection development profile and effective, open communications between vendor and the library. Universities change; programs change; peo- ple change; the emphasis changes. If the library is depending en- tirely on a profile in developing a contract with the vendors, it should plan to change its description as often as deemed necessary.

Since there is no blueprint for the perfect approval plan, each library must review its own experience and determine whether ap- proval plans are successful; each library must arrive at its own unique decision.

A library starts a plan in the first place for its own reasons: it may hope for a more efficient acquisitions procedure, or it may hope to relieve subject bibliographers of routine selection; or it may have other purposes in mind. After the plan is in operation, a library must then evaluate the plan in the unique setting of that library and no other.

It is apparent that all acquisition librarians have to abide by the limitations of their institutions and that they are subject to some control by the faculty. However, the ideology of an approval plan program appears to be sound and shows the possibilities of bringing in a wide variety of useful materials.

REFERENCES

1. Peter Spyers-Duran, ed., "Approval and Gathering Plans in Academic Libraries," (Littleton, CO:Libraries Unlimited, 1969):ii, 142.

2. Peter Spyers-Duran and Daniel Gore, eds., "Advances in Understanding Approval and Gathering Plans in Academic Libraries," (Kalamazoo, MI:Western Michigan University, 1970):vi, 220.

3. Peter Spyers-Duran and Daniel Gore, ed., "Economics of Approval Plans," (Westport, CT:Greenwood Press, 1972):x, 134.

4. Peter Spyers-Duran and Thomas Mann, Jr., eds., "Shaping Library Col- lections for the 1980's," (Phoenix, AZ:Oryx Press, 1980):[xii, 235p.].

5. Ian W. Thom, "Some Administrative Aspects of Blanket Ordering," *LRTS* 13, no. 3 (Summer 1969):338-342.

6. Harriet K. Rebuldela, "Some Administrative Aspects of Blanket Order- ing: A Response," *LRTS* 13, no. 3 (Summer 1969):342-345.

7. Ian W. Thom, "Some Administrative Aspects of Blanket Ordering: Re- joinder to a Response," *LRTS* 13, no. 3 (Summer 1969):345-346.

8. William Oxford, "The Economics of a Domestic Approval Plan," *College & Research Libraries* 32 (September 1971):368-375. [Paper was originally delivered at the Third International Seminar on Approval and Gathering Plans in Large and Medium-size Libraries, February 17-19, 1971, West Palm Beach, Florida.]

9. Linda Ann Hulbert and David Stewart Curry, "Evaluation of an Approval Plan," *College & Research Libraries* 39, no.6 (November 1978):485-491.

10. Dennis E. Newburn and Irene P. Godden, "Improving Approval Plan Performance: A Case Study," *Library Acquisitions: Practice and Theory* 4, no. 2 (1980):45-155.

11. Anna H. Perrault, "A New Dimension in Approval Plan Service," *Library Acquisitions: Practice and Theory* 7, no. 1 (1983):35-40.

12. J. H. Reidelbach and G. M. Shirk, "Selecting an Approval Plan Vendor I: A Step-by-Step Program," *Library Acquisitions: Practice and Theory* 7 (1983): 115-122; J. H. Reidelbach and G. M. Shirk, "Selecting an Approval Plan Vendor II: Comparative Vendor Program," *Library Acquisitions: Practice and Theory* 8 (1984);157-202; J. H. Reidelbach and G. M. Shirk, "Selecting an Approval Plan Vendor III: Academic Librarian's Evaluations of Eight United States Approval Plan Vendors," *Library Acquisitions: Practice and Theory* 9 (1985):177-260.

13. K. A. Schmidt, "Capturing the Mainstream: An Examination of Publisher-Based and Subject-Based Approval Plans in Academic Libraries," in Danuta A. Nitecki, ed., *Energies for Transition: Proceedings of the Fourth National Conference of the Association of College and Research Libraries*, 1986, 93-95.

14. Kathleen McCullough, Edwin D. Posey and Doyle C. Pickett, eds., *Approval Plans and Academic Libraries* (Phoenix: Oryx, 1977).

15. Sul H. Lee, ed. *Acquisitions, Budgets, and Material Costs: Issues and Approaches* (New York: The Haworth Press, Inc. 1988).

16. R. C. Wittenberg, "The Approval Plan: An Idea Whose Time Has Gone? And Come Again?" [Presented at the 1987 Charleston Conference on Acquisitions] *Library Acquisitions* 12, no. 2 (1988):239.

17. *Ibid.*, pp. 240-242.

18. Peter B. Kaatrude, "Approval Plan versus Conventional Selection: Determining the Overlap" [at the University of California at Los Angeles Libraries] *Collection Management* 11 no. 1-2(1989):145-50.

19. Approval Plans in ARL Libraries, Systems and Procedures Exchange Center, Association of Research Libraries, (Washington, D.C.:The Association, 1982). (SPEC Kit:83)

20. Approval Plans/Systems and Procedures Exchange Center, Association of Research Libraries. (Washington, D.C.: The Association, 1988). (SPEC Kit:141)

21. *Ibid.*

22. Kathleen McCullough, Edwin D. Posey and Doyle C. Pickett, eds., *Approval Plans and Academic Libraries* (Phoenix: Oryx, 1977), 136-145.

23. *Ibid.*

24. *Ibid.*, pp. 123-132.

Approval Plans:
The Multi-Vendor Approach

Peggy Chalaron
Anna Perrault

SUMMARY. Since approval plans were first offered in the mid-1960's as an alternative acquisitions method to title-by-title selection and firm ordering, they have become the predominant method of library acquisitions. The literature on approval plans follows several major themes: pro/con the merits of approval plans; how to choose the right vendor; and vendor performance studies. Less frequent topics include specialty approval plans; surveys of approval plan use; and bibliographies of approval plan literature. The majority of articles treat the approval plan as a one-dimensional topic, i.e., as if all libraries have only one approval plan and vendor when in actuality many libraries' total approval program involves the use of several vendors. This article reviews the literature with respect to the maintenance of multiple approval plans. The experience at Louisiana State University which has maintained a multiplicity of approval plans for thirteen years is described. The studies and re-examinations of the multi-vendor approach conducted throughout the years at LSU are detailed. Current technological developments in the delivery of approval plan services are covered. The future impact of these developments are considered for what changes they may bring to long-established approval plan patterns in many libraries.

Approval plans have been an accepted, and indeed the preferred, method of acquiring currently published monographs since the late 1960's. In the early years of their existence, approval plans for English language publications were offered by several major U.S.

Peggy Chalaron is Head, Acquisitions, and Anna Perrault is Head, Interlibrary Services, Louisiana State University Library, Baton Rouge, LA 70803.

and British vendors. Foreign language publications were commonly obtained through blanket orders, not approval plans. Two factors came to distinguish approval plans from blanket orders: (1) direct shipment books could be returned; (2) a plan could be structured with a combination of direct shipment and notification forms. The notification form produced by computer output was not a feature of the more comprehensive but inflexible older blanket order system.

In the beginning, approval plans did not gain instantaneous acceptance and there were articles and programs debating their advantages and disadvantages. With large increases in publication rates and library budgets in the 1960's, approval plans began to take over the acquisitions field because they simplified the job and made it less time-consuming. A measure of their acceptance is that not only did approval plans come to be used as the predominant acquisitions method in all types and sizes of libraries, but also nearly every European vendor doing business in the U.S. began to offer approval plan programs. A few U.S. vendors which had concentrated on supplying English language publications expanded to begin offering foreign language publications. A number of companies developed approval plans for specialized subjects or types of publications, such as childrens' books or small press books.

THE LITERATURE OF APPROVAL PLANS

One measure of the acceptance and preeminence of approval plans is the number of conferences and published articles devoted exclusively to this subject. Rossi's "Library Approval Plans: A Selected, Annotated Bibliography," is an overview of the history of the development and literature of the approval plan field. This bibliography of seventy-seven entries covers the time span from 1957 to 1987. The articles are from thirty-five different journals and a number of volumes of conference proceedings.[1]

In the early years, the literature of approval plans was filled with articles arguing the merits of approval plans from the economic standpoint; from the efficiency standpoint; and from the point of view of the selector, the user, and the acquisitions staff. Another predominant theme in approval plan articles was the comparison of vendor services conducted to choose the most suitable vendor for a particular library. It was not until 1981 that Reidelbach and Shirk codified this process in the definitive article on the subject, "Selecting an Approval Plan Vendor: a Step-by Step Process."[2]

As approval plans gained wide acceptance, debates over their desirability gave way to articles on management and evaluative performance studies. The first surveys of approval plan users were also conducted in the early 1970's. The first ARL Spec Kit on approval plans was published in 1982. After maturing into an accepted and dominant methodology for library acquisitions/collection development, a methodology which had stood the test of numerous studies, there was a tapering off of the number of articles dealing with approval plans in the latter half of the 1980's.

USE OF MORE THAN ONE VENDOR

Throughout the evolution of the approval plan from an alternative method of acquisitions to the predominant method of acquisitions in the majority of academic and many public and school libraries, the literature gives the impression that all libraries deal with only one approval plan vendor at a time. There are very few articles which treat approval plans from a multi-vendor, multi-disciplinary, or multi-layered approach. One exception is a paper given at the First ACRL national conference in 1978 by Posey and McCullough, who authored several publications dealing with approval programs. This paper describes the movement at Purdue from one comprehensive approval plan to several departmentally controlled approval plans.[3]

There are a number of articles which conduct comparison studies using more than one vendor but no significant accounts of the long-term maintenance of multiple approval plans. The only study on the use of multiple plans is a recent paper by Barker given at the Charleston Conference in 1988. "Vendor Studies Redux: Evaluating the Approval Plan Option From Within," is an account of an evaluation of over forty separate approval plans which were being maintained at the University of California, Berkeley.[4]

Although the body of approval plan literature gives the impression that approval plans are a matter of selecting one vendor, there are a few indications that the picture is more complex for many libraries than simply the use of one vendor.

The first surveys of approval plans in libraries are in the early 1970's. In his survey of blanket order and approval plans in ARL libraries, Dudley found that the number of plans in a single library ranged from one to forty.[5] Since no distinction was made between the blanket order and the approval plan in the survey, it is likely that the larger numbers occurred in libraries with many separate blanket orders for foreign acquisitions.

One of the first comprehensive surveys devoted exclusively to approval plans was conducted by McCullough, Posey, and Pickett. The results of the survey were published and analyzed in a monograph, *Approval Plans and Academic Libraries*. This survey specifically excluded any type of foreign language or publisher plans. All of the questions in the survey are framed in the singular, and the question is not asked if the respondents currently operate more than one domestic approval plan.[6]

A survey by Leonhardt and Sitts in connection with the first ARL Spec Kit on approval plans published in 1982 did ask the libraries responding to indicate how many approval plans were in place. Of the total number of plans in effect in the libraries responding to the survey, 31.1% were domestic and 68.9% were foreign. Divided into the two categories of domestic and foreign plans, the average number of domestic plans per library was three, and ten for foreign plans.[7] While the preponderance of the literature is concerned with domestic plans, this survey indicates that foreign plans make up a larger percentage of the approval program of academic libraries.

Five years later the Spec Kit was updated by Sitts and Howard. A similar survey revealed that approval plans were utilized by 93.6% of the responding libraries, up from 85% in the first survey. The domestic plans made up 35.9% and the foreign 64.1% of the approval plans. Of the libraries with approval plans, 86.2% had both domestic and foreign approval plans with the number of plans for a single library running the gamut of from one to seventy.[8]

The results of this survey of academic libraries proves false the impression left by the majority of the literature that libraries maintain *an* approval plan. True, the most common type of plan is the general/multi-subject, all purpose plan which accounted for 48.2% of the total of all types of plans. The special subject type of plan had 33.6% of the total.[9] But these breakdowns only further illustrate that the growth of numbers and types of approval plans had made them a very complex acquisitions activity by 1988.

Of the ninety-four libraries responding to the 1988 ARL survey, 71% report using more than one domestic plan, with a high of twenty-five plans in one library. Fully 34% reported either two or three plans. The foreign plans ranged up to fifty-two in one library, but one to three plans were reported by 38% of the libraries.[10]

Thus, it can be safely asserted that a library with more than one domestic approval plan and an additional number of foreign approval plans is not atypical. The approval plan program at Louisiana State University would seem to exemplify this pattern of more than one domestic approval plan accompanied by a number of foreign plans.

THE APPROVAL PROGRAM AT LOUISIANA STATE UNIVERSITY

In 1977, blanket orders at Louisiana State University with individual university presses were consolidated into approval plans with two vendors, one for North American and one for British imprints. This was the beginning of the multi-vendor approval program at LSU.

In 1978 and 1979, with a newly formed collection development division, English language approval plans, excluding university press publications, were begun with three more vendors. At that time, collection development had just been centralized into three positions of a bibliographer each for the humanities, the social sciences, and the sciences. The approval plans were divided accordingly with each bibliographer choosing a different vendor and setting up a profile for the subjects under his/her jurisdiction. There was consultation among the three bibliographers to structure the approval plans to prevent overlap and duplication in materials supplied. The university press approval plan was treated internally as a blanket order, with review by the selectors only of titles judged by acquisitions staff to need review.

A few years later, another approval plan was set up with a British vendor for British imprints. Separate foreign language plans for German, French, Italian, and Iberian imprints followed. With the addition of a small number of very restricted special plans, the total number of vendors and plans in effect ten years later was nine.

REASONS FOR THE MULTI-VENDOR APPROACH

There were several reasons for setting up English language approval plans with more than one vendor at LSU. They can be divided into the two major categories of acquisitions and collection development, the two areas that all approval plans must satisfy if business is to continue over a long span of time.

(1) *Acquisitions*. There are advantages in not having too large a portion of the total acquisitions business with any one vendor. LSU began shifting toward approval plans in the late-1970's because of increases in the library materials budget and in world publication output. At this time, the breakup of the Richard Abel company had left a lingering apprehension with many acquisitions librarians that engendered caution for not having one's entire current order file disappear into a void overnight.

Multiple approval plans can be utilized to distribute the work load among several employees. An interactive triangular relationship can be formed with one selector and one acquisitions employee dealing with each other and one vendor. Having only one selector to work with in relationship to a particular dealer can simplify approving shipments and other aspects of the functioning of the approval plan. It is not necessary to sort shipments by subject or selector, or to wait until a number of people have reviewed a shipment.

Another attractive reason to acquisitions for having more than one vendor was the possibility of comparing vendors for various aspects of service, discounts, etc. It would be possible to conduct "real" studies from actual approval plan receipts, instead of simulated studies using shipments of notification slips.

(2) *Collection Development*. The main reason the selectors were interested in multiple vendors is obvious; the use of multiple vendors gave each selector total autonomy. Each selector could establish a separate profile and not have that profile affected every time another selector made profile changes.

The multi-vendor approach does not force individual bibliographers to all work with the same dealer whether they are comfortable with that dealer or not. This approach allows better and more specific coverage than that of an across-the-board plan. Each selector can monitor the vendor's adherence to the profile and other performance aspects of the approval plan.

In an academic library, the division of approval plans by selector and vendor can give the faculty a sense of identification with the approval plan. The faculty know the selector they deal with is in direct control of the approval plan for their subject area.

It is easy to understand the reasons individual selectors would be in favor of separate approval plans. But from the acquisitions point-of-view, it would seem that multiple plans would create more work dealing with so many different vendors. There is the possibility that multiple plans could cause higher return rates if the profiles are not tightly drawn or the vendor's interpretation of the profile is not strict.

Multi-vendor approval plans could have a negative impact on vendor discounts; however, had LSU combined the three subject approval plans, the total volume would not have been sufficient to increase any one vendor's discount. Discounts have been 10%, 12-16%, and 13% for science, humanities, and social science plans, respectively. Informal analyses of discounts over a period of time have shown few changes, but other factors have been apparent. For example, the humanities plan utilizes a sliding rather than a flat discount because humanities subject areas generally have higher publisher discounts. The social sciences discount has been eroded by state laws which involve taxing the parent company. Thus, discounts must be considered in tandem with a variety of factors unique to each library.

APPROVAL STUDIES AT LSU

In the 1960's LSU experimented with a small university press plan with Richard Abel, but by 1966 had established direct blanket orders with almost 90 different university presses. These blanket orders worked well from the standpoint of coverage and timeliness of receipts, but paperwork was escalating and discounts, once generous, were beginning to decline. An approval plan seemed a reasonable alternative, but closing that many accounts and merging them into one approval plan would be a monumental task. Although a few libraries were already using a similar plan, LSU was reluctant to make a change of this magnitude without a comprehensive study. Five vendors supplied bibliographic forms for a six month period to simulate an approval plan. These forms were compared with actual receipts from the presses in terms of profile coverage, receipt time, discounts, and processing requirements. Two vendors closely replicated the direct shipments and the other three were in an acceptable range. Vendors had the added attraction of bibliographic forms provided with the books, consolidated shipments, and less paperwork.[11] Since a university press or publisher approval plan was a viable option, vendors were selected for plans with few restrictions.

While there have been profile changes throughout the years since the multi-vendor approach was first inaugurated at LSU, the approval program for English language imprints has remained as initially set up with the same four major vendors. There have been a number of studies conducted at LSU over the years on various aspects of approval plans. These were performed either as on-going monitoring of return rates or for limited time spans to check discounts, etc.

The acquisitions department began to monitor returns in 1978/79 and has constant data for a ten-year period.

In Table I, return data for the decade 1978/79 – 1988/89, the university press plan shows a negligible rate of return for the entire period. This low return rate is due to the difference in profiling between the university press plan and the three large subject plans. The university press plan as initially set up has few exclusions; only in the past five years when budgetary difficulties set in has there been more strict review of the university press imprints.

In 1978/79, the three major subject plans were each placed with one of the largest U.S. approval plan vendors. The first year return rates were near the top of the acceptable range for returns. (Although vendors will tolerate return rates in the double digits, at LSU anything over 10% has been regarded as too high.) Experience with the plans and some tinkering with the profiles, such as switching of troublesome areas from direct shipment to forms, brought returns down to a very acceptable rate for all three vendors.

It is easy to look at the return data and read in changes in staffing

TABLE I

Return Rates as Percentages of Receipts

Fiscal Year	Soc Sci	Sci	Humanities	Univ Press
1978/79	7.27	11.64	9.18	1.04
1979/80	5.60	8.96	4.31	0.96
1980/81	7.51	7.14	4.17	1.14
1981/82	7.15	4.71	4.59	0.44
1982/83	8.34	10.60	3.66	0.15
1983/84	8.95	9.06	5.29	0.31
1984/85	10.60	8.00	6.48	1.16
1985/86	13.22	8.38	4.64	0.42
1986/87	12.79	1.55	9.66	0.39
1987/88	19.80	19.41	9.80	2.20
1988/89	11.08	22.04	14.68	5.99

and funding patterns. For the first six years, funding increased and then stabilized. The social sciences plan was expanded, with the other two remaining as initially set up. The social sciences return rates begin to climb beyond the 10% range in 1984/85 when a larger number of selectors, all of whom had not set up the profile, began to review the approval plans. The humanities and science plans maintained a steady rate for two years until a further reorganization of collection development responsibilities in 1986. Another factor at work, simultaneously with the change in personnel monitoring the approval plans, was that funding began to drop at the same time. Thus return rates are showing a steep rise by 1987/88, reflecting a narrower approach to spending funds because of budgetary restraints.

Although data had been maintained continuously on return rates, a study had not been made of the reasons titles were being returned.

When the return rate began to climb in 1985/86 with a larger number of less experienced selectors reviewing approval plans, a study of books returned as a duplicate to the same title supplied on another plan was begun in 1986. Table II shows the return rate of duplicates as a percentage of all returns for each of the three plans.

The main discovery when the returns were analyzed was that duplicates to other approval plans made up a low percentage of overall returns. Even the high of 20% in the humanities in 1986/87 is not a large proportion of all returns.

Not unexpectedly, the data from the duplicate returns shows a clustering of returns in a few subjects with interdisciplinary aspects that can variously be approached from a social sciences, a science, or a humanities angle. The B's which have both religion and psychology are one of the areas in which maintaining separate approval plans can cause overlap problems. When books are profiled, not just according to a suggested LC classification, but also according to subject headings, psychology titles can be described so that the computer matches them to both psychology and medicine profiles. In the same way, certain areas in sociology and social welfare can match up with religion or medicine. The history and philosophy of a subject can pop up in philosophy, history, or the subject.

When the humanities returns which are duplicates to other approval plans are analyzed for the three year period, the B and the PS classifications together account for from sixty one year to one hundred percent another year of the humanities duplicates returned. While it is easy to explain overlap between profiles for the B's, the duplication of an area as straightforward as literature is mystifying.

TABLE II

Duplicates to Other Approval Plans as Percentage of Overall Returns

Fiscal Year	Soc Sci	Sciences	Humanities
1986/87	5.37	14.92	20.22
1987/88	.69	4.57	10.02
1988/89	.60	.73	2.70

Likewise, in the sciences for the three year period, the Q's and the RJ's together make up from fifty to one hundred percent of the science duplicate returns. The social science duplicates are fairly evenly distributed in the BF, D, H, J, and LB classifications.

What Table II does not illustrate, but can be ascertained from looking at the raw data, is that there are several patterns which point out the practices of the individual dealers in their subject profiling. Tied in with this is the data on the supply time-frame of the individual dealers. In looking at the raw data, one of the highest return rates is caused by the shipment of titles which fall within the primary profile responsibilities of one vendor but were supplied first by another vendor. The vendor shipping the titles first was profiling titles to "fit" many subject categories which were actually mainstream material for the later vendor's primary subject coverage. But because the title had already been supplied by the first vendor, the duplicate was returned to the second vendor which actually should have been supplying the title. This data confirmed opinions about the profiling techniques of the vendors which had long been observed, but not systematically studied. It is possible to observe differences in profile philosophy and practice by utilizing more than one vendor, even if for different subject profiles.

Although the profiling at LSU was carefully structured to minimize overlap between plans, a certain amount was bound to occur. In the first six years of the return statistics, the low rates testify to the careful profiling. The three recent years show that a large number of the returns are in areas which are susceptible to profile matching in more than one subject. The experience at LSU with multiple-vendor/subject plans proves that such an approach is workable, but can very easily be tipped out of kilter by profile adjustments.

A large portion of the overall returns is not accounted for by duplication between vendors. There are many different reasons for return based upon the judgment of the reviewer. The analysis of these other returns had no relationship to the multi-vendor approach to approval plans.

One fairly common pattern in which libraries have utilized more than one vendor has been to maintain a separate approval plan with a British vendor for British imprints. At LSU the humanities approval plan was split between the domestic vendor and its British counterpart. The profile was not exactly the same, the British profile being more restrictive than the domestic one. Several years later, a similarly restrictive social sciences plan was added with the same British vendor.

Prior to the addition of the social sciences plan, a study was made of the coverage of British imprints by the on-going social sciences and university press approval plans as compared with the coverage supplied by the British dealer. The study, utilizing forms from the British vendor to compare with actual receipts, was begun in 1983 and continued for six months. The results showed the British vendor's coverage to be 30% more titles than the American vendor had treated.[12] Ferguson reports on a similar study in "British Approval Plans: American or British Vendor." Ferguson also found that the British vendors supplied a larger number of titles than the American vendor — 16.8% more in 1983 and 19.8% more in 1985.[13] The difference in the percentage of British imprints between the Ferguson studies and the LSU study are probably due to the differences in the profiles of the two libraries.

FUTURE CONSIDERATIONS

Although there have been organizational restructurings, budgetary fluctuations, and personnel changes at LSU, the multi-vendor approval plans approach has continued to the present almost exactly as it was initially set up in 1977. While the total approval plan was originally customized to the organization of the collection development division, the long-established plans were continued with the same vendors because the plans had proven to be satisfactory. Continuing the same approval plan program in the future may be contingent upon factors other than service, discount, and satisfactory profile coverage. As approval plans have become increasingly popular, vendors have evolved similar standards in these areas and differences have become less and less apparent. Developments in library automation may dictate another look at the maintenance of a number of separate plans with different vendors. The two primary considerations will be the vendor's ability to keep abreast of technology and the library system's ability to readily accept that technology.

At the ALA Midwinter Conference in January 1987 the RTSD RS Automated Acquisitions/In-Process Control Systems Discussion Group's program was titled "Use of Approval Plans with Automated Acquisitions." Three speakers, two vendor representatives and one academic librarian, discussed utilization of vendor-supplied, machine-readable records for approval plan materials; vendor-provided records could be loaded directly into an automated acquisitions system. Gibbs' "LC MARC Approval Tapes at Auburn University" provides a detailed look at the procedure developed there for loading vendor tapes into the NOTIS system.[14] Smith's "Linking Approval Plans and Automated Library Acquisitions Systems" describes the process from the vendor viewpoint.[15] Options included either a full LC MARC cataloging record or an abbreviated MARC format record created by the vendor, but in 1987 not all vendors had both options. However, three years later the options are broader and continuing to expand.

Telephone interviews in the spring of 1990 with representatives of LSU's four major approval vendors determined that all now offer machine-readable records to accommodate numerous libraries with a variety of commercial and local acquisitions systems. A recurring theme was the need for industry standards that would provide quality control, consistency, and reliability. One vendor representative stressed that the book vendor is a product service vendor who cannot get ahead of the automated systems vendor, so librarians must communicate their needs and wants to both.

All of the vendors are predicting more and more electronic transmission services and on-line dial-up access to databases providing a variety of approval information. On-line access will replace and expand the microfiche services now being provided. Maddox gives a humorous account of some possibilities in "Are the Gods Listening?"[16] Not only will it be possible to determine the status of a title, but it will also be possible to take action which will initiate an appropriate procedure such as claiming or firm ordering. The automated approval plan of the near future will consist of records supplied by tape or telecommunications and another component of supplementary services for on-line inquiry, claiming or ordering.

Adapting manual procedures to multiple approval vendors is a relatively simple process handled within the Acquisitions Department. Adapting automated procedures requires testing which has a far-reaching impact on the library's Automation and Systems office, the campus Computer Center, and the liaison between the two. After testing, what are the implications of dealing with four tape loads from four vendors as opposed to one? Are there idiosyncrasies that will impact automation and computer personnel on an on-going basis? Budgetary contingencies have prevented LSU from testing and/or utilizing vendor-supplied, machine-readable records. However, it is conceivable that the answer to these questions could alter the present multi-vendor approval plan program at LSU and other libraries.

REFERENCES

1. Rossi, Gary J. "Library Approval Plans: A Selected, Annotated Bibliography." *Library Acquisitions Practice and Theory*, v. 11, no.1(1987), 3-34.

2. Reidelbach, John H. and Shirk, Gary M. "Selecting an Approval Plan: A Step-By-Step Process." *Library Acquisitions Practice and Theory*, v.7, no.2(1983), 115-122.

3. Posey, Edwin D. and Kathleen McCullough. "Approval Plans One Year Later: the Purdue Experience with Separate School Plans." In *New Horizons for Academic Libraries: Papers Presented at the First National Conference of the Association of College and Research Libraries*, Boston 1978. New York: K.G. Saur, 1979, p. 483-489.

4. Barker, Joseph W. "Vendor Studies Redux: Evaluating the Approval Plan Option From Within." *Library Acquisitions Practice and Theory*, 14, no.2 (1989), 144-141.

5. Dudley, Norman. "The Blanket Order." *Library Trends*, 18(January 1970), 318-327.

6. McCullough, Kathleen, Edwin D. Posey, and Doyle C. Pickett. *Approval Plans and Academic Libraries: an Interpretive Survey*. Phoenix, AZ: Oryx Press, 1977.

7. *Approval Plans in ARL Libraries*. (SPEC Kit, no.83). Washington, D.C.: Association of Research Libraries, 1982. pp. 2-3.

8. *Approval Plans*. (SPEC Kit, no.141). Washington, D.C.: Association of Research Libraries. 1988. p. 9.

9. Ibid.

10. Ibid., pp. 7-8.

11. Chalaron, Peggy. "Acquisition of University Press Books: an Approval Plan Simulation." Unpublished report, LSU, 1976.

12. Bensman, Stephen J. "Social Sciences Bibliographer Annual Report, 1982/83." pp. 2-3. Unpublished report, LSU, 1983.

13. Ferguson, Anthony W. "British Approval Plan Books: American or British Vendor?" *Collection Building*, v.8, no.4, 18-22.

14. Gibbs, Nancy J. "LC MARC Approval Tapes at Auburn University." *Library Acquisitions Practice and Theory*, 11, no.3(1987), 217-219.

15. Smith, Scott A. "Linking Approval Plans and Automated Library Acquisitions Systems." *Library Acquisitions Practice and Theory*, 11, no.3(1987), 215-216.

16. Maddox, Jane. "Are the Gods Listening?" *Library Acquisitions Practice and Theory*, 11, no.3(1987), 209-213.

A Comparison
of Two Approval Plan Profiles:
A Study in Success and Failure

Sally W. Somers

SUMMARY. Approval plans are commonly used by academic libraries as a method of collection development. At the heart of each plan is the individual library profile which is developed for each library and determines what materials will be sent. Although the profile is crucial to the success or failure of a plan, its role in determining a library's level of satisfaction or dissatisfaction with the plan has not been examined. Does the profile define and enforce the library's wishes or does it serve to raise expectations? Two ARL libraries, the University of Georgia and Tulane University, for a time had university press approval plans with the same book jobber. Each organization had vastly different profiles and completely different reactions to their plans. Although unique circumstances on each campus played a role in the outcome of each plan, it appears that the profile served its stated purpose well — it defined wishes and also set expectations.

Approval plans are firmly entrenched in the majority of academic research libraries as a method of adding designated categories of books to the collections. Plans can be publisher or subject based, can be restricted to either domestic or foreign publications, or a combination. In the small library with few staff who are involved with selection, an approval plan frequently serves as a way to easily acquire basic materials. By contrast approval plans in large research libraries may be instituted for a variety of reasons: to ensure that the "basics" are collected systematically so that selectors may concen-

---

Sally W. Somers is Assistant University Librarian for Technical Services at Howard-Tilton Memorial Library, Tulane University, New Orleans, LA 70118.

trate their efforts on selecting in greater depth for specific subject area(s); to permit them to have more time to review and to weed the collection; or to provide coverage in hard-to-fill subject areas. Few research libraries limit themselves to just one approval plan regardless of the size of the collection management staff.

Book jobbers, both domestic and foreign, offer approval plans to fill every need. Although specifics may vary slightly from vendor to vendor, each handles approvals in a similar way. Domestic vendors routinely have staff, including an approval plan manager and bibliographers, whose sole responsibilities lie with approval plans. Generally the approval plan manager makes presentations to libraries considering adopting a plan and also monitors the work of the approval plan staff. Bibliographers are responsible for profiling books and also may be responsible for handling customer service for specified clients. Profiling is done with book-in-hand and involves assigning the appropriate subject descriptors using a thesaurus developed in-house and assigning non-subject parameters.

At the heart of any approval plan is the individual library profile. As vendors are quick to tell librarians, each profile is constructed to meet the individual library's needs and desires so that the acquisition of titles becomes easier and faster. Although each vendor's completed profile may vary slightly, individual documents generally contain the same elements: subject descriptors and non-subject parameters. Based on each library's expressed wishes, books will be shipped whenever these two elements intersect. In theory if the profile accurately reflects the library's collecting patterns and future desires and the vendor ships the books within a reasonable time period, there should be a high degree of satisfaction with the approval plan.

COMPARISON OF PROFILES

For a time two Association of Research Libraries libraries, the University of Georgia and Tulane University, had university press approval plans with the same vendor. The vendor is a large, highly-respected book jobber with many research library clients and hundreds of approval plan customers. If one measures the level of satisfaction by the number of books received and the comments and/or complaints of selectors and of faculty then the results of each plan were vastly different. One organization was so strongly dissatisfied that the approval plan ultimately was moved to a vendor who proved to be better able to fill that library's needs while the other was and remains a very satisfied customer.

What were the causes for the markedly different reactions of each organization? What role did the profile play in raising or lowering the collective expectations of each collection management staff? Did each library's profile merely formalize previously set expectations or was the profiling of titles one ingredient which, added to these expectations, set the stage for one plan to fail and the other to succeed? Was what became a significant set of problems for one library caused by vendor error? Or was their established procedure for handling publisher-associated problems rejected by one organization and accepted almost unquestioningly by the other?

The profile for the University of Georgia Library could best be described as "wide-open." Selectors at UGA wanted very few exclusions based on either subject or nonsubject categories. In keeping with this approach the subject descriptors portion of the profile enumerated each major subject division with no areas excluded. Examples of subject categories included "Fine Arts Division" or "Humanities Division" with all subcategories to be included automatically. Nonsubject exclusions were kept to a minimum. Exclusions comprised only undergraduate texts, reprints, and books with media. All books in series whether the first volume or subsequent volumes and volumes within monographic sets after the first volume were to be shipped—no forms were desired. Price limitation was high with notification required only for those titles costing over $250.00. In essence the profile was intended to be simple and straightforward so that any title published by one of these presses, except undergraduate texts and reprints, would come as part of the approval plan. Bibliographers expected to tell the teaching faculty that titles published by this important category of publishers could be expected to reach the library within a short time after the date of publication.

By contrast the Tulane profile was a great deal more detailed and complex. Tulane had no intention of garnering large numbers of books across the spectrum. Instead this institution wanted to collect in carefully specified subject areas. The profile initially encompassed only the social sciences and humanities, with the sciences added several years later. Within each of these broad categories the profile was and is tightly drawn. When compared to the wide-open Georgia one, the contrast is starkly apparent. Rather than broad subject descriptors such as "Literary Texts Division" or "Applied Interdisciplinary Social Sciences Division" meant to include everything, it is obvious that each descriptor was considered and evaluated on an individual basis by the Tulane staff. Although books in the "Applied Interdisciplinary Social Sciences Division" were included, subcategories such as "Crime and Criminals Division" were blocked. Similarly just as books profiled in the "Literary Texts Division" were included, subcategories such as "Epigrams and Anecdotes" were excluded. Although nonsubject parameters were not as tightly profiled, this portion of the profile also reflected the same careful attention to detail. Lower-level undergraduate texts, popular collections, reprints, pamphlets, and popular biographical treatments were eliminated. Price limits were set at $100.00 with forms required for titles exceeding that amount. As an additional restriction books in numbered series after the first volume were not to be sent automatically.

Since each profile demonstrates its university's radically different approach to their approval plan, how well did each profile fulfill the expectations of each organization? How satisfied was each organization with its plan?

University of Georgia

If there ever was an approval plan that appeared to be easy to fulfill, the University of Georgia's wide-open plan seemed to fit this bill. All a vendor needed to do was to procure all the books from the university presses and ship them to Georgia, almost in a pass-through fashion. It would appear that very little profiling of any title was needed and that aspect of vendor services could be largely ignored for Georgia. Actually in practice this was not the case. Since the vendor profiled the titles as part of the standard procedure for all approval plan clients, the resulting profiling caused titles which UGA selectors expected to be shipped to be excluded, largely because of the assignment of nonsubject parameters. Of particular difficulty was the category of upper- and lower-division college texts. Agreement as to what constituted an undergraduate college text was never reached between the vendor and UGA bibliographers. In most instances titles were considered textbooks by the vendor which were considered monographs by the Georgia librarians and teaching faculty.

The amount of time that the vendor spent on profiling proved to be troublesome. Where the vendor prided himself on careful profiling done *only* with book-in-hand, this time was viewed as something of a hindrance at UGA because it slowed shipment. Teaching faculty were told routinely that virtually all titles with a university press imprint would come on the approval plan and that they should reach the library faster than if they had been firm ordered. Often this did not happen. The expectation of quick delivery complicated the scenario because the delay of any title, whether it was excessive or not, added fuel to the smoldering discontent of the selectors and the faculty.

The common vendor practice of selectively short shipping customers when the vendor failed to receive the requisite number of copies to fill his orders proved to be particularly troublesome. Although in theory vendors apply this on a rotating basis to all approval plan customers, analysis of titles never shipped to Georgia indicated that, in this case, the University may have been hit excessively. Once a title was not shipped as part of the original shipment, it was later discovered that many never were shipped.

Tulane University

But what of Tulane with its closely defined approval plan? Although on the surface this plan seemed to be the more difficult to service, expectations of the bibliographers appeared to be much lower. In general there seemed to be a feeling of relief on the part of both the collection managers and the acquisitions staff that a significant segment of collecting could be counted on to come automatically. Tulane had experienced a period of significant growth in its materials budget and the relatively small collection development and acquisitions staffs had some difficulty in firm ordering the larger quantities of materials needed to spend these funds. Since university press titles were habitually firm ordered, an approval plan would allow this important category of materials to reach the library relatively easily.[1]

Because coverage of university press titles was not expected to be comprehensive, the question of missed titles never was significant. Books that had not arrived in the library and were needed on a rush basis simply were firm ordered. Requests to claim a title that was expected to come as part of the approval plan simply never materialized.[2] When faculty inquired about whether or not a title would come on approval, selectors carefully explained the profile and firm ordered if they deemed it necessary. As long as the title could be obtained, faculty seemed to be satisfied.[3] Selective short shipment was not an issue as long as it was passed equally among all approval plan clients, and apparently it was in Tulane's case.[4]

The Tulane approval plan remains in effect today with the original vendor. Both selectors and the acquisitions staff view it as very successful and the level of satisfaction remains very high. In this case the profile seems to mirror accurately Tulane staff desires and to reflect the atmosphere of the University.

CONCLUSION

Since both of these are research libraries which agreed that university press titles are an important category of materials that each wanted to acquire routinely, and the vendor was one who had a proven reputation for providing good service to academic libraries, what factors caused such radically different reactions to each approval plan? Although the response of the two organizations represents varied and complex sets of circumstances unique to each campus, it is fair to assume that the profile did play a part in the success of the Tulane plan and the failure of the University of Georgia plan.

Conversations with staff at Tulane about their plan quickly reveal their delight at its implementation; their desire to collect in rather narrowly-defined subject areas; their satisfaction with the profiling techniques of the vendor and the subsequent coverage; plus the overall satisfaction of the Tulane teaching faculty with the plan.[5] The fact that Tulane maintains a strong liberal arts program focused on the humanities and social sciences which are disciplines that are not as heavily dependent on the most current research and publication may account for the calmer, less demanding attitude of the faculty and of the selectors. Although research and publication are required for tenure, the smaller student body has not mandated the hiring of significantly large numbers of junior-level faculty who are hungry to publish so they will be eligible to gain tenure at the end of their seven years.

At the mention of the possibility of vendor error by short-shipping or missing titles completely the Tulane staff seemed to display an almost forgiving attitude and to think that chances of this occurring were somewhat unlikely.[6] Little monitoring of the titles supplied on the plan had been undertaken nor was it anticipated. Generally staff seemed to accept the widely-held view that the vendor's excellent reputation was deserved. The fact that virtually no complaints were received from faculty or graduate students seemed proof to them that the plan worked as anticipated. There was little need and no interest in comparing service among book jobbers.

In Tulane's case the profile seems to have accurately defined expectations and to have enforced them as well. The Tulane experience probably represents an example of an almost perfect match between vendor, approval plan, and library.

Examination of the University of Georgia's experience reveals a vastly different experience.[7] Implementation of the expanded university press approval plan was an occasion for great joy among the UGA selectors because a full-blown plan had been strongly desired for several years.[8] As the land-grant institution in the state, the University of Georgia Library served a highly diverse teaching and research program. Although the liberal arts program was large and strong there were a number of professional schools as well as strong science and agriculture programs, each expecting to receive materials as part of the approval plan. Speedy delivery was expected from all vendors for all types of materials and the approval plan was to be no exception.

Much of the pressure on the selectors came from the teaching faculty and the large numbers of graduate students. It was commonplace for members of either group to come into the library to inquire about an expected title. On that large state-supported campus with its emphasis on a strong publications record as a prerequisite for tenure there were significant numbers of junior-level faculty in tenure-track positions who were eager to meet these requirements. Senior faculty frequently were just as impatient and as demanding regarding acquiring new materials, largely because they had impact on their current research.

Whenever a title had not been shipped in what was deemed the appropriate amount of time, some of the selectors seemed to believe that essentially they were viewing the tip of an iceberg. If one title had not come as quickly as expected it was highly likely that many more either were slow or were being missed altogether. Because of this belief some bibliographers regularly monitored their subject areas and, in many instances, their suspicions were confirmed — titles were being missed.

The University of Georgia experience represents a classic mismatch in terms of services rendered and level of satisfaction just as surely as the Tulane experience represents the ultimate degree of satisfaction between client and vendor. As a result of the loss of the Georgia account the vendor reportedly instituted a "quick and dirty" method of profiling in order to satisfy customers who were not interested in precise subject description and just wanted the books. In stark contrast to Tulane's forgiving attitude whenever titles might be missed, the Georgia selectors were unforgiving, largely because of the ire they faced from faculty and graduate students. The Georgia bibliographers expected all books to come rapidly and when they did not, the level of dissatisfaction grew to truly epic proportions. Had the level of expectation been lower and had the vendor not made repeated errors — first in short shipping UGA a disproportionate number of times and then in missing titles when additional stock was received — the relationship might have been salvageable, and the overall experience less disastrous. The end result was extremely painful for both organizations.

In both of these instances each profile served the purpose for which it was intended — it defined the library's wishes for the approval plan and reenforced the organization's level of expectation. As the designated instrument it served its purpose well.

REFERENCES

1. Interview with Floyd Zula, Head of Acquisitions, Howard-Tilton Memorial Library, Tulane University, March 13, 1990; Interview with Daniel R. Todd, Chief Bibliographer, Howard-Tilton Memorial Library, Tulane University, March 13, 1990.

2. Zula interview.

3. Todd interview.

4. *Ibid.*

5. Todd interview; Zula interview.

6. Todd interview.

7. As Head of the Acquisitions Department at the University of Georgia from 1979-1989, the author has first-hand knowledge of these happenings and was actively involved with the collection development staff and with the vendor during all the stages of the plan—profiling, implementation, problems and complaints, comparison study with another vendor, and actually moving the plan to the second vendor.

8. Prior to this time the approval plan had been restricted to seven of the largest university presses.

Approval Plan Profiling
in the Small Academic Library

Gary J. Rossi

SUMMARY. Approval plans have generally been limited to the medium to large size university or research library. Should librarians in small college libraries wish to consider the feasibility of an approval plan, there are circumstances unique to that type of institution which may require a different approach to subject profiling than would be the case in the larger libraries. The discussion centers around a case study of the Mansfield University Libraries' experience with subject profiling an approval plan in selected disciplines.

Over the course of the last thirty years or so, the use of approval plans has spread so that they now have a secure position in the acquisitions programs of many academic libraries. The professional literature of the last thirty years has reflected this evolution.[1] In the early days, we find many discussions of the advantages and disadvantages of the approval plan concept from a philosophical point of view. More recently however, we find attempts to lay the groundwork for situating the approval plan in the realm of day-to-day practice.[2] Although the approval plan concept has spread to more academic libraries, it has been almost totally limited to medium and large university and research institutions as opposed to small colleges. There are numerous reasons outlined in the literature that explain this phenomenon but which are outside the scope of this paper. One recent article by Hunter Kevil, however, seeks to dispel the generally regarded idea that approval plans are workable only in the larger institutions.[3] Kevil's two fundamental premises are that

Gary J. Rossi is Automation Librarian/Cataloger, Main Library, Mansfield University, Mansfield, PA 16933. He was previously Humanities Librarian with collection development responsibilities.

approval plans are " . . . underutilized by academic libraries generally and by college libraries in particular . . . " and that " . . . the root difficulty underlying the low incidence of approval use stems from imperfect perceptions of what an approval plan can and cannot do, from lack of knowledge of how to make the plan work and derive maximum benefit from it." The purpose of this paper is to continue this train of thought with respect specifically to the development of the approval plan profile which is without question the key to ultimate success or failure of this type of acquisitions program.

SMALL ACADEMIC LIBRARY ACQUISITIONS PROGRAM

It is necessary to place this discussion of approval plan profiling in the context of the acquisitions program of a typical small college. The following is based on experience at Mansfield University and observation of other college libraries. A typical book acquisitions budget may vary between $75,000 to $150,000 or more and may be subject to considerable fluctuation from year to year depending on the economic health of the college, unless there is in place an agreement with the college administration that the budget will not decrease below a certain floor. This "book" budget may also need to be stretched to buy non-print materials such as phonodiscs, videocassettes and other audio-visuals.

The small college library must orient its material selection policy toward the primary aim of the parent institution, which is for the most part undergraduate teaching rather than graduate level and faculty research. Students must be provided with materials that support the assignments given by faculty and faculty must be supported in their preparation for teaching.

Probably the most difficult reality that those who select materials for a small college library must deal with is that, unless the college is richly endowed, selection must aim at developing the breadth of the collections rather than any one area in any depth. This becomes all the more apparent when one considers the fact that many colleges offer the same breadth of academic programs as do larger institutions. The same basic "core" collections for the various academic disciplines need to be developed. To complicate matters, some colleges may have certain star academic programs that attract a number of students out of proportion to the majority of the other departments. Since allocation formulas usually take into account student enrollments to some degree, these relatively larger departments will likely get a greater share of the pie at the expense of the smaller departments whose "core" collection may suffer.

Responsibility for the selection of materials for the small college rivals the issue of the amount of money available from year to year. Usually there is some degree of cooperation between librarians and classroom faculty and ultimate responsibility may reside with either group. When librarians are responsible for the greater part of selection duties they usually turn to such publications as *Choice*, *Library Journal*, or other library oriented review media as well as scholarly journals. With a limited budget to cover all the college's curricula, individual selection decisions become more and more important and hence a greater reliance on reviews.

A word or two needs to be said on the subject of staffing the acquisitions department. There usually exists a relatively small staff including a mix of professionals and paraprofessionals who are responsible for both decision making on the placement of orders and monitoring the status of outstanding orders, for claiming and other necessary follow up, and for fund accounting. Hard to get items not supplied by the major vendors or that are not channeled through the same pre-order verification routines such as music scores, sound recordings, small press imprints, audiovisuals and microcomputer software, for example, risk falling through the cracks for lack of sufficient time to follow up on all unfilled orders. The acquisitions process like many other library routines is very labor intensive and its success depends heavily on the intelligence, stamina, and creativity of the staff.

THE APPROVAL PLAN PROFILE – GENERALITIES

Perhaps the most crucial aspect and key to the success of an approval plan is the subject profile. There may be little gained and considerable damage done if a library enters into an approval plan without careful consideration of its profile. The development of the profile in cooperation with the approval plan vendor becomes in effect an exercise in determining the library support needs of each of the academic programs to a fairly high degree of specificity. Some of these considerations must include a survey of the subject content of course offerings, of the intervals in which these courses are taught and their approximate enrollments, and of the nature of the assignments given to students by the faculty. The profile becomes a mirror image of the college's collection development policies but in greater detail.[4]

The approval plan vendor usually supplies lists of subject descriptors. For each subject descriptor, the library chooses either to receive books on that subject automatically, to receive bibliographic slips instead of books automatically, or to receive nothing on that subject. The profile may be entirely subject based or may include directions on certain publishers to specifically include or not. In this way undesirable publishers can be eliminated and certain known high-quality publishers in one or more subject areas may be singled out for special treatment. In addition to subject and publisher criteria, other modifiers such as academic level, place and language of publication, editions, geographical content, price, or special types of publications such as bibliographies or study and teaching materials may be chosen.

THE APPROVAL PLAN PROFILE – SPECIFICS AND CASE STUDY

The following discussion will relate the process undertaken at Mansfield University to profile selection requirements with one of the major United States approval plan vendors. First, a short description of the University will be provided.

The University enrolls approximately 3200 full and part-time students, including about 250 students in its graduate programs in education, art, music, home economics, and psychology. Undergraduate programs are offered in the traditional liberal arts and sciences disciplines. Pre-professional programs in education, criminal justice, business, and computer science are among the most highly enrolled programs. On average the acquisitions budget for books and other non-serial type material has remained at about $100,000 over the last several years. Library facilities consist of a Main Library and two branch libraries, one for music and the other for education. The total bound volume count is about 210,000.

The professional library staff in the public services division are subject specialists and act as liaison to academic departments. Each subject specialist has either a master's or doctoral degree in a subject area in addition to the professional library degree. Subject specialty areas are humanities, social and behavioral sciences, natural sciences and mathematics, business and English, music, and education. Selection practice up to the time of implementation of the approval plan consisted of librarian selection from *Choice* and *Library Journal*, from publishers' announcements, from scholarly journals, and from recommendations by classroom faculty. As might be imagined from a group of professionals well educated in a subject discipline, there was a certain amount of resistance to give up some control over selection to an approval plan vendor.

Several compromises were made. First, not all subject areas were to be included in the approval program and, second, the librarian selectors had the option of deciding for each area included in the approval plan the percentages of the total dollar allocation to be spent via the approval plan and via the traditional firm order method. Those subject areas that were to be included in the approval plan were defined as those for which the plan by itself would most likely bring in the highest percentage of titles that otherwise would have been selected by the firm order method. On the other hand, subject areas identified not to be included in the approval plan were those in which a narrowly focused part of total book production (e.g., military science, economics) or areas that could not be supplied by the approval plan because of publisher or subject considerations (e.g., music therapy).

Once this initial definition of what would and would not be included in the approval program was agreed upon, the profiling task began. The subject descriptor lists were divided among the subject specialist librarians for them to indicate whether books, slips, or nothing were to be received. Modifier sheets were also completed about which more will be said later.

One subject area to be profiled was history. The approval plan vendors design their subject descriptors around their observation and study of college and university curricula. However, in an admirable attempt to cover all areas commonly taught at colleges and universities in the United States, there arises necessarily a bias toward comprehensiveness that favors institutions that are attempting to cover most of their current acquisitions via one or more approval plans. This is one of the primary reasons why the commonly held belief that approval plans work only in larger libraries has remained convincing. But it does not necessarily have to be so.

Let us examine in some detail the subject descriptor list for the history of Western, Central, and Eastern Europe.

Europe — History

Western Europe — History

    Great Britain — History

    Great Britain — History — Tudor and Stuart (1485-1714)

    Great Britain — History — 19th century

    Great Britain — History — 20th century

    Ireland — History

    France — History

    France — History — Revolution and Napoleonic Empire (1789-1815)

    Italy — History

    Spain and Portugal — History

    Scandinavia — History

Central Europe — History

    Germany — History

Germany — History — Third Reich (1933-1945)

Eastern Europe — History

Russia — History

Russia — History — 1917 to present

There are ostensibly gaps in coverage. Great Britain has the most detailed treatment, France is covered in two descriptors, and the history of Spain and Portugal of all times is treated together in one descriptor. This should not be surprising, however, because as mentioned earlier, these subject descriptor lists aim at comprehensive treatment. If a topic is not considered to warrant a specific descriptor it will most likely be contained under a more general one.

This situation has bearing on the issue of breadth vs. depth mentioned earlier. For example, Mansfield teaches courses in all the areas in the descriptor list except Scandinavia and Ireland. But it also teaches about areas such as the Austro-Hungarian Empire which, because it lacks a specific descriptor, would be contained under the broader heading Central Europe. So in order to retain some breadth it was necessary in this case to profile all subjects except Scandinavia and Ireland. We did not want nor could we afford financially to receive all books on these topics. We did, however, need to have the opportunity to see what is being published in order to select the most appropriate titles. The result was that, in general, we chose to receive books for specific subject descriptors that cover areas in our curriculum and to receive bibliographic slips for broader descriptors that cover areas both taught and not taught. After experience with book and slip receipts, revisions were necessary based upon the same general parameters. While it may be said that selecting from bibliographic slips diminishes the advantage of the approval plan concept, we were able to return unwanted books which came as a result of slip selection. The problem of not having the chance to see books that were *not* selected from slips remained unresolved, however, but is basically the result of the kind of trade-off inherent in any type of materials selection method.

Another profiling issue involved the use of subject descriptor modifiers. As mentioned previously, there was with our approval plan the opportunity to modify any subject descriptor according to certain qualifiers. The following were the modifiers:

1. Academic level (undergraduate, graduate, etc.)
2. Publishers (university press, trade, etc.)
3. Place of publication
4. Language of publication
5. Editions (first, subsequent)
6. Physical format
7. Continuations
8. Subject development (bibliography, biography, etc.)
9. Textual format (readings/anthologies, etc.)
10. Geographic designator
11. Price

By carefully profiling these modifiers it was possible to narrow the subject descriptors to varying degrees of specificity. For some areas it was necessary to develop more than one modification pattern. For example, in the field of art it was necessary to have two geographic designator patterns, one for studio topics and a second one for history topics. Since the studio courses were aimed primarily at the art of the United States, Great Britain, and Western Europe, the geographic designator pattern for studio topics was restricted to receive books treating only these geographic areas. This would clearly not work for art historical topics since the University offered instruction in the history of art of the United States, Great Britain, and Western Europe in addition to the art of Latin America, Eastern Europe/USSR, the Near East/North Africa, South and Southeast Asia, Africa, the Far East, and Oceania.

The modifiers for academic level also presented some challenges. Among the expected levels were undergraduate, graduate, and professional. In addition, undergraduate and graduate were again broken down into two "selected" categories which are defined to mean the best of each group. It must be understood that these categories are all mutually exclusive. For example, selected undergraduate is not included in undergraduate. Since, in practice, the "selected categories" by themselves turned out to be rather restricted, the decision to limit to those categories initially resulted in too few books. The remedy was to profile for the undergraduate category as well.

Another aspect of the modifier for academic level that needed to be considered was the issue of graduate vs. undergraduate. It is fair to say that the difference between the definition of these two levels may vary considerably in practice from one institution to another. In the case of mass communications, for example, we had profiled for undergraduate and selected undergraduate but received relatively few books. By adding graduate level to that profile we began to receive a greater number of books that turned out to be more satisfactory for our needs.

Another important aspect of profiling was consultation with classroom faculty. Once the profiles were completed in draft form they were shared with each of the academic departments in order to elicit comments and suggestions for modifications and to gain their support for review of the on approval books once shipments would begin. The initial fear that faculty would overprofile was not realized. There was an understanding of the budgetary limits and for the most part faculty were conservative in their suggestions.

A final aspect of profiling that deserves mention is that of the return rate of books that arrive automatically as a result of the profile but that are not wanted for various reasons and subsequently returned. Most approval plan vendors have a range of percentage return rates within which they are comfortable. This range is ostensibly based on pure business considerations. It is easy to understand that as more books are returned the cost of doing business with the library rises. The important thing to realize as it relates to college libraries with limited budgets is that for some subject areas it may not always be possible to reduce the return rate to a level suggested by the approval vendors just by adjusting the subject profile, the modifiers, or some other variable. This dilemma may be resolved by the vendor's computation of the overall return rate rather than by holding each subject discipline to the prescribed rate. In this way, one area's high return rate may be offset by another discipline's low rate. Vendors may be willing to work with the library toward a goal that benefits both the library and the vendor over time. This is why it is important to work closely with the vendor's representative from the beginning of profile development and to share information about the changing needs of the library as they develop.

CONCLUSION

An approval plan may definitely be a viable option for a small college library. It must be emphasized, however, that the profile must be continually monitored so that it accurately reflects the changing information needs of students and faculty. A carefully constructed and closely monitored profile is the key to a successful approval plan that respects both the sometimes idiosyncratic needs of the library and the business exigencies of the vendor.

REFERENCES

1. For a review of the literature see this author's "Library Approval Plans," *Library Acquisitions: Practice & Theory*, 11(1), 1987, pp. 3-34.

2. For recent and comprehensive research findings on the scope and use of approval plans in academic libraries see the series of three articles published in *Library Acquisitions: Practice & Theory* by John H. Reidelbach and Gary M. Shirk, "Selecting an Approval Plan Vendor: a Step-by-Step Process," 7(2), 1983, pp. 115-122; "Selecting an Approval Plan II: Comparative Vendor Data," 8(3), 1984, pp. 157-202; "Selecting an Approval Plan III," 9(3), 1985, pp. 177-260. There are also two handbook-like monographs on the practical aspects of approval plans: Jennifer S. Cargill and Brian Alley, *Practical Approval Plan Management*, Phoenix, Ariz.: Oryx Press, 1979; and *Approval Plans in ARL Libraries*, Washington, D.C.: Association of Research Libraries, Office of Management Studies, 1982.

3. L. Hunter Kevil, "The Approval Plan of Smaller Scope," *Library Acquisitions: Practice & Theory*, 9(1), 1985, pp. 13-20.

4. Noreen S. Alldredge, "The Symbiotic Relationship of Approval Plans and Collection Development," in Peter Spyers-Duran and Thomas Mann, Jr., eds., *Shaping Library Collections for the 1980's*, Phoenix, Ariz.: Oryx Press, 1980, pp. 174-177.

Library/Vendor Cooperation in Collection Development

Lauren K. Lee

SUMMARY. Collection development efforts can often be enriched by cooperation with materials vendors. Libraries often lack the staff, time, or automated systems required to carry out collection development activities efficiently and effectively. Vendors are currently offering a number of generic and customized selection services. These services can be used by all types of libraries for a wide range of materials, including current publications, retrospective books, audio recordings and videos. They may be used for ongoing selection or for special projects. Various approaches are possible, each with its own set of advantages and disadvantages. Libraries can profit from these methods if they are informed consumers, investigating the options and actively participating with the vendor in designing and using the service.

A library's collection development efforts can often be enriched by well-planned cooperation with materials vendors. During the typical labor-intensive process, individual titles must be identified, evaluated, searched against holdings, selected, checked for availability, and ordered. All too frequently, libraries lack the professional staff, support staff, or time to carry out each step efficiently and effectively. They may also lack the automated systems to check titles quickly or to manipulate data readily. More and more vendors are now offering both generic and customized selection services which assist libraries in the functions listed above. They are often able to create selection lists from their existing database of titles,

---

Lauren K. Lee was formerly Collection Management Administrator for the Atlanta-Fulton Public Library. She is now Manager of Collection Development Services for the Brodart Company.

181

availability information, and order frequency information, or to create new databases of titles from review sources, bibliographies, or listings supplied by the library.

These lists can be useful in a variety of settings, from developing a specific subject area in support of a new degree program to building an entire collection for a new facility, or from targeting a particular format to providing consistent coverage of new titles. Academic libraries have long known the value of approval plans for current selection. Public library systems, who frequently create their own selection lists for their member branches, can perhaps use a vendor's help in compiling these lists. In the last ten years, a number of public library systems have been fortunate enough to have embarked upon significant expansion programs and have often relied on vendors' assistance in building their opening day collections. Vendors who specialize in materials for the school market also provide these "opening day" services in addition to supporting curriculum trends and state award programs.

Vendor-assisted projects are also applicable for many different areas of the collection including current publications for ongoing selection, retrospective books in specific subject areas or for new collections, and audio and video materials.

CURRENT SELECTION SERVICES

Many vendors provide newsletters, announcements, and catalogs of new and forthcoming titles. These tend to be of limited usefulness, often appearing to be more like advertisements than recommendations. They can be interesting items for browsing, but rarely make a significant contribution to collection development. Librarians rely most heavily, of course, on review sources for their current selection information. Many vendors use the standard sources (e.g., *Booklist, Choice, Library Journal, School Library Journal*) in some way, from basing their own buying decisions on them to "indexing" titles in their database with review citations. Vendors to school libraries, in particular, seem to offer lists of recommended titles pulled from review sources. In the future perhaps it will be possible for a library to receive new title information from a vendor or publisher through disks or downloading of information into the library's own automated acquisitions system. This data could then be reviewed and manipulated into a selection list or an order.

Returning to the present, approval plans are probably the most common form of collection development service provided by vendors. Many academic libraries rely heavily on the books supplied by their approval vendor. If the plan has been profiled carefully, the vendor has performed conscientiously, and the library has had consistent funding, then the plan will help systematically develop the collection, while saving the library countless hours of new title identification, pre-order searching and order preparation. Certain standing orders and blanket orders with publishers can offer similar benefits.

Some vendors can also offer listings based on their own sales history for types of titles, for a particular period, or to a specific market. This is, of course, most appropriate for collections of popular materials, where general popularity of an item is an accurate predictor of popularity in one's own library. Vendors who cater to both the library and the retail trade are perhaps best able to provide this kind of information. Some are also willing to provide libraries with lists of titles suggested for bookstore inventory. Other vendors will provide print-outs of their own inventory, so that a library can maximize the initial fill rate if that is important.

RETROSPECTIVE COLLECTION DEVELOPMENT

In retrospective collection development librarians must first identify which titles are standard or have been recommended, then check those titles to find out which are still in print. Once again, vendors may be able to help in both areas. As with review sources, some "index" their title databases with standard bibliographies (e.g., *Children's Catalog*, *Public Library Catalog*, etc.). The last edition of *Books for College Libraries* was made available on machine-readable tape. Libraries that can make use of that technology can purchase it directly and check it against their own holdings, but those who can't do so can work through vendors for the same result. Some vendors are also able to generate customized lists for libraries, combining titles from multiple sources into a single listing.

A key factor, however, is the vendor's ability to update availability information readily. A library using a print bibliography must check each title against *Books in Print*. A vendor, by necessity, keeps its title database constantly updated with the latest status information received from publishers. A listing produced by a vendor, therefore, can include availability information or be limited to those titles still officially in print.

Other methods of vendor-assisted retrospective collection development make use of a library's own database of holdings. Some libraries might want to run an automated check of their holdings against titles in a bibliography. If they can supply machine-readable records of their holdings, some vendors will perform the matching and produce a listing of titles in the bibliography not held by the library. Boyd Childress discussed the option of matching a library's machine-readable holdings against a vendor's MARC file to identify titles available but not held by the library (Childress 141). Or, a library might want to reproduce the collection of one branch to create another branch. A vendor can then take machine-readable holdings records, treat them as an order, supply those titles that are available and report those that are not.

It is the author's own experience with a large special collection development project that piqued this interest in library/vendor cooperation. In 1985, the Atlanta-Fulton Public Library passed a bond referendum to build ten new libraries, renovate and/or expand three more, and reinstate extension services. Also included in this program was $9.4 million for materials for the opening day collections, totalling over 500,000 items. From a practical standpoint, it was clear that library staff could not identify, search, select, order, receive, catalog and process all these items in the short period of time available while still conducting business as usual.

It was decided that the library would contract with a vendor for collection development lists; the acquisition of the books themselves; cataloging, processing and database services; and storage of materials until the buildings were completed. Even if all the additional services had not been required, the selection lists were reason enough to work with a vendor. The strategy was to develop a group of well-rounded, comprehensive lists that included titles from a variety of sources, arranged in shelflist order, with availability status noted. There were eight primary lists — adult fiction, adult nonfiction, adult reference, juvenile picture books, juvenile easy books, juvenile fiction, juvenile nonfiction, and juvenile reference. The adult nonfiction list was the masterpiece of the project, containing over 45,000 titles from 34 bibliographies, selected publisher catalogs, replacement lists developed previously by the Library, and the vendor's sales history files. The lists were designed to emphasize popular, practical, public library materials and to maximize the fill rate by focusing on identifying the best of what was available (rather than waste time agonizing over out of print classics). The Library sought to obtain everything possible from the contract vendor, but also recognized the need to deal with a number of "must order direct" publishers, particularly for reference materials. At this writing, all but four of the libraries have opened. The consensus is that the collections, which ranged from 5,000 to 80,000 new volumes, were strong and systematically built, much more so than would have been possible from purely local efforts.

Many other public and school libraries around the country have had or begun expansion programs similar to AFPL's and have used vendor assistance in varying degrees. It is usually possible to get lists sized by the number of volumes ultimately desired or by the budget available. Children's titles can usually by separated or coded by age range or grade level. Most vendors also offer to provide "de-duplicated" lists (i.e., a title appears on the list only once even though cited in more than one source) or to block duplicate orders generated from multiple lists.

RECORDINGS

Collection development for audio recordings can also benefit from library/vendor cooperation. Many of the same benefits described above apply, but there are some additional complications to the audio arena. Not only is there a wide range of types of materials—from classical to contemporary music, New Age to rap, and, in spoken word recordings, from unabridged Shakespeare to an abridgment of the latest bestseller—but there are also a variety of formats—the moribund LP records, cassette tapes and compact discs. Bibliographic control has also been more difficult for libraries due to the lack of a true *Books in Print* equivalent and to producer numbers which somehow seem less user friendly than ISBNs. Therefore, a knowledgeable audio vendor can help bridge the gap between the universe of recordings and the library's collection. At least two vendors offer automatic shipment programs of new recordings based on various *Billboard* charts. Others provide listings of titles by category (e.g., "Operas-Complete," "Operas-Highlights," "Film/Show Music") and/or in-stock listings from their warehouse. Another possible approach is for the library to mark a *Schwann Catalog* and send it to a vendor as a glorified order form. For spoken word recordings, catalogs from the major producers can also be used effectively for large orders.

The library video scene is a rapidly changing one. Where once there was a dearth of review sources, now there seems to be a plethora. Perhaps soon the "standard set" of video review sources will become apparent. In the meantime, however, catalogs from library and retail vendors are a common source of order information. They vary in quality and in the amount of information provided on each title, but they do perform the important function of announcing upcoming and new releases. At least one review source is interacting with a vendor by noting which reviewed titles are carried by the vendor. Other approaches include an automatic shipment program of top videos and a listing of the videos that have sold best to libraries in a specific period of time. As with audio, the video spectrum is broad. It is difficult for a library or a vendor to handle popular features in the same way as educational titles. Perhaps even more so than in other subject areas, a "film literate" video selector is needed to interpret vendor catalogs, know producers' reputations, and recognize the difference in two productions of the same title.

ADVANTAGES AND DISADVANTAGES OF VENDOR-ASSISTED SELECTION

Obviously, the approaches described above, and variations of them, have advantages and disadvantages for the library consumer. On the plus side, they are efficient in that they delegate mainstream title identification and routine availability checking to the vendor, thereby freeing librarians for other tasks including, but not limited to, more careful evaluation of the titles offered or searching for more esoteric titles. A substantial amount of selection can be accomplished in a relatively short time. As Douglas Duchin aptly said, "In essence when you hire a jobber you are hiring extra librarians" (Duchin 18). Next, the costs are minimal since most vendors provide these services free of charge especially if the library uses the tools to make purchases with the vendor. Also, the fill rate is usually higher than the norm since the vendor has checked availability and knows ahead of time the titles that the library may purchase. Added services may also be available, such as cataloging and processing, database updating, storage, or even shelving. And, finally, these methods are synergistic in that by combining the librarians' skills and the vendors's knowledge, they result in a better collection than either party could have developed independently.

One potential disadvantage of some of these approaches is that the selectors may not be able to see as much evaluative information as they would like. To some, it may feel like buying blind. And, in some cases, mistakes may be made — an abridged edition or a boxed gift set may be received. Each library has to set its own tolerance level for errors and weigh that against the benefits of any approach.

These methods also tend to be collection-centered rather than client-centered. The vendor is working from bibliographies, review sources, and knowledge of the entire market or segments of it rather than from familiarity with a library's community and its needs. As Lundin has said of public libraries, "Public libraries need to be aware of their readers and to select and evaluate with a balanced view: a delicate balance of community needs and bibliographic authority" (Lundin 111). It is up to the library, not the vendor, to provide this balanced view.

One temptation with these methods is to rely too heavily on them, letting them become the sole or primary collection development activity. The library must remember that these methods may have their place in selection activities, but they need to be constantly re-evaluated and supplemented with more traditional selection practices.

QUESTIONS FOR VENDORS

Should you decide to seriously consider one or more of these methods, be sure to do your homework. You should be able to articulate your needs and the desired results to the vendor. You will probably want to ask several vendors questions about the services they provide, so that you can compare the options and make the best choice. Listed below are a series of questions that would be appropriate for investigating vendor-generated selection lists:

- How quickly can the vendor produce the list?
- Is it a generic list or one customized for the library?
- Is there any charge or purchase obligation?
- What sources will the vendor use to create the list? Can the library select from a group of sources or recommend additional ones?
- How will the list be arranged? — by Dewey number? LC number? Author? Title? Subject category? If in call number order, is a title index available?
- What elements of information will be shown for each title?
- How many titles will be included? What is the approximate dollar value?
- Can the list be restricted by age level, publication date, binding, or other criteria?
- Will the list include out-of-print titles and/or must order direct titles?
- Can the library review the list before accepting it?
- Is there a required or suggested time frame for placing orders from the list?

These questions are just a starting point for dialog with vendors. The answers to many of these questions will depend on decisions made jointly by the library and the vendor as they go through the process.

If the vendor has answered your questions satisfactorily and you have decided to proceed, do so with confidence and optimism, but keep the following in mind:

1. If creating a list or automatic shipment program, choose your sources carefully. Know what is in them and if you indeed want it.
2. Know the difference between sources that list items without qualitative judgment and sources that recommend titles. Distinguish between them as you make use of the sources.
3. Don't expect the vendor to read your mind. If your library never buys Nancy Drew books, tell the vendor that or don't be upset when those titles appear on a list based on sales history.
4. Read through selection lists and familiarize yourself with them before marking any orders. Ask the vendor to explain anything you don't understand.
5. Don't abdicate your responsibility. Be an active participant in designing the process or project and in making use of the tools provided.
6. Choose the vendor and product that best suits your needs. Vendors' capabilities and specializations vary. Check the references of libraries that have used similar products. Talk to the vendors' staff members and gauge their collection development expertise.
7. Expect and demand solid results, but not miracles. Understand what is and isn't possible. Get what you can from a project and move on to the next logical step. One-stop shopping may be convenient but it won't provide the best collection. To quote Duchin again, "If you want a successful program, you must let the vendor do what a vendor does best. Let him buy the new and obvious titles and leave collection development, in the truest sense of the word, to the library" (Duchin 19).

CONCLUSION

Vendors are becoming more savvy about collection development services and how to offer them to the library market. It is safe to say that the options in this area will continue to increase, in both the scope of print services available and in the possibilities for electronic services. Libraries can profit from these services as long as they are knowledgeable consumers. Cooperation between the two parties can only lead to improved library collections.

REFERENCES

Childress, Boyd and Nancy Gibbs, "Collection Assessment and Development Using B/NA Approval Plan Referral Slips," *Collection Management*, 11(1/2) 1989, 137-143.

Duchin, Douglas, "The Jobber as a Surrogate Acquisitions Librarian," *Library Acquisitions: Practice and Theory*, 7, 1983, 17-20.

Lundin, Anne H., "List-Checking in Collection Development: an Imprecise Art," *Collection Management*, 11(3/4), 1989, 103-112.

Using an Economic Development Approach to Improve Budget Forecasting Techniques, Collection Allocation Methods, and Library Budgeting Decisions

Glen J. Kelly

SUMMARY. This article focuses on library funding patterns, forecasting and collection budget allocation methods. The inadequacy of previous forecasting models and allocation formula used at Laurentian are detailed. The importance of using different techniques for forecasting and allocating in times of decreasing or static collection budgets are emphasized. The implications and impact of outside government or agency funding on library budget allocations and planning decisions are examined. The author concludes that:(1) Ascertaining trends or cycles in government or agency funding can lead to an improved method of forecasting future library collection budgets; (2) Collection development methods and allocation formula that work well in times of increasing budgets have to be re-examined when budgets are cut, or remain the same; (3) Taking an economic development approach will incorporate a wider variety of factors into the decision process used to allocate collection funds.

Laurentian University is located in Sudbury, Ontario, and was founded in 1960. The University is a bilingual institution, providing services to Anglophone and Francophone populations residing

Glen J. Kelly is Assistant Director, J.-N. Desmarais Library, Laurentian University, Sudbury, Ontario, Canada P3E2C6.

throughout Northeastern Ontario. The main campus library currently possesses a collection of over 800,000 items, including Canadian and Ontario government publications which are received on deposit. The library subscribes to approximately 3,000 current subscriptions. Collection funding has increased during the decade of the eighties from $340,000 in 1980-81, to $1,255,000 in 1990-91. Approximately 85% of the total university funding is received from the Ontario Government, 10% from student fees, and 5% from private, corporate or other governmental donations and grants.

The question of equitable allocation methods for collection funds at Laurentian has been a perennial problem identified by management as early as 1970, when the impact of Provincial Government cutbacks were first felt. It was during the 'lean' years that a different approach to selection, allocation, and budgeting decisions had to be made to incorporate a wider variety of overall factors into the decision process used to assign collection funds. The references detailed in this article are based on the 'lean' years of the seventies, and do not reflect current collection budget growth patterns. The first part of this article deals with the specific problems faced by Laurentian and the formula attempts that were made to find a more equitable method of dividing the collection budget. The second part deals with the theoretical framework and what was developed to provide a more comprehensive collection decision-making model for forecasting and allocating collection funds.

PART 1:
THE PROBLEMS FACED BY LAURENTIAN

To understand the tight budget years faced by Laurentian during the 1970's, it is necessary to examine the financial environment of Ontario's universities. Each year, the Ontario government provided operating grants to the universities on the basis of enrollment-based formulas, with various program weights which, with only minor modifications, remained the same during the decade. Under this formula, universities received a higher Basic Income Unit (B.I.U.) or grant for a Master's or Doctoral student than for a student in a general Bachelor of Arts program. Special assistance grants were also provided to the small emerging universities; however, these grants were gradually reduced and discontinued.

Throughout the 1970's, the value of the Basic Income Unit was decided by the Provincial Government, not on what it actually cost the universities to offer programs, but on how much the government felt they should spend on the universities. In real dollar terms, Provincial Government spending increased; but, in constant dollars "after correction for inflation, the per student income of the Ontario universities in 1974-75 was only 85% of the level five years earlier."[1]

Early in the seventies, enrollment began to decline at Laurentian. As a result, the university was forced to rationalize and establish new operating budget priorities by applying operating income on the following basis: (1) to salaries and wages of the staff; (2) to develop new programs to meet the changing needs of the student population; (3) to provide for an expanding role as a regional university, supporting 27 off-campus centre programs spread over a 400-mile radius of Northern Ontario; (4) to maintain the physical resources of the university, which included the physical plant and other operating costs; (5) to maintain an adequate library service and collection to meet the research needs of the faculty and the community.

A block allocation formula was established by the Senate Budget Committee for the internal division of operating income. In 1978-79, the library's block allocation was $1,100,000. The Senate Library Committee, in conjunction with the Chief Librarian and Library Department Heads, then decided the actual distribution of the block allocation. The priority in distributing the library operating budget in that year was: (1) to staff salaries; (2) to fixed costs: services like CODOC (Co-operative Government Documents Project), I.U.T.S (Inter-University Transit System), essential office supplies and service contracts; (3) to collection purchasing; (4) to purchases of new equipment and non-essential supplies.

The collection budget used to purchase library materials from 1970 through 1979 remained static at $300,000! During the same period, the salary budget and other fixed costs increased by 7.5% annually. The total library staff complement decreased from 59 full-time equivalents to 39. A variety of formula were proposed to allocate the dwindling collection budget between the disciplines in a 'fair and equitable' manner, however, the formula attempts ended in failure.

FORMULA ATTEMPTS AT FINDING A SOLUTION

The first attempt at using a formula to distribute the collection budget was initiated in 1973. A simple mathematical formula was designed, using the total collection budget: subtracting annual standing order commitments, common fund commitments and periodical subscriptions, and dividing the remaining funds by the number of students in each discipline. The formula failed to meet the approval of the various disciplines as it did not take into account the use of library materials, and no allowance was made for the average price of materials in each discipline.

The second attempt in 1976 focused on faculty complement and student enrollment factors, but made no attempt to face the huge escalation in the price of current subscriptions: from $40,000 in 1970 for 4,000 titles, to $140,000 for 3,500 titles in 1976.

The third attempt in 1979 was based on a more sophisticated mathematical formula. A score was computed for each discipline on the basis of the nine categories listed below. These categories or factors were then used to determine a weighted index for the division of the library collection budget.

1. Average price of books   Points

    — below $20.00   0
    — $20.00 to $25.00   1
    — $25.00 and over   2

2. Average price of periodicals

    — below $20.00   0
    — $20.00 to $75.00   1
    — over $75.00   2

3. Need for books as determined by use of book budget

   — 1977-78 book budget overspent by $200.00 or more 2
   — 1977-78 book budget approximately in balance 1
   (less than $200.00 left or overspent)
   — 1977-78 book budget underspent by $200.00 or more 0

4. Need for books as determined by nature of discipline

   — use of current library books essential to this discipline 2
   — a need for some important library books 1
   — library books of peripheral importance
   to the discipline 0

5. Need for periodicals determined by the use now made
   of periodicals

   — periodicals in library used regularly 2
   — periodicals used moderately 1
   — periodicals not used very much 0

6. Need for periodicals as determined by the nature of the
   discipline

   — current periodicals essential to the discipline 2
   — some current periodicals useful to this discipline 1
   — periodicals not particularly important 0

7. Priority accorded to this discipline in 1978-79
   University Budget

   — redundancies 0
   — teaching complement reduced 1
   — teaching complement increased or maintained 2

8. Student enrollment as per student/courses

   — below 400 0
   — 400-700 1
   — 700 and above 2

9. Graduate program

   — yes 2
   — no 0

The total budget was then to be divided by the total point count which would give a unit dollar amount to each point. The various disciplines would then be allotted money based on their total point count. The above formula, although it attempted to take many important factors into account, was soundly criticized for the weighting given to each of the factors. It was rejected primarily on the basis that the formula did not represent the average cost of material to each discipline fairly. A discipline like Chemistry with an average periodical cost in 1979 of $174.88 did not feel that the use of the proposed formula reflected a fair method of distributing collection funds.

The fourth formula developed during the 1970's was in response to the third, and attempted to weight the average cost of materials in each discipline more adequately than the previous formula. The fourth formula was simplified to include only four factors for each of the disciplines:

1. Average Book Price
2. Average Periodical Price
3. Usage based on actual expenditures on books and periodicals and circulation statistics expressed as a percentage
4. Faculty complement and student enrollment

The steps to be followed in calculating the amounts were: (1) *Average Book Prices × % usage + Average Periodical Price × % usage × Faculty and Student complements = Total point count.* (2) *Total Collection budget divided by point count = individual amounts for each discipline.* This formula was considered 'fairer' than formula three; however, it involved too radical a departure from former collection budgets distributions and was rejected.

Final budget distributions during the period mentioned were actually decided, not on the basis of formula, but primarily on political and historical factors. This allocation method maintained the status quo and, in its favour, did take two important factors into account that the other formula attempts did not: the politics of the budget decision-making process, and the history of past budgeting procedures.

One significant change did take place during the search for a formula. The current periodical fund, which had been considered a common fund expense until 1978-79, was divided by discipline. This effectively meant that most of the Science disciplines, who until this point had received the majority of the collection funds, were forced to stop buying new materials as inflation used up their allotments at a faster rate than other disciplines.

DEVELOPMENT OF A COLLECTION BUDGET ALLOCATION AND FORECASTING MODEL

After many years of attempting to find a formula, I began to ask one basic question: Can a formula or model be found with enough universality to be used to allocate funds between the various disciplines in a university? A significant body of library literature exists on formula and allocation models.[2] One comment that gets to the root of the problem is from the field of management science. C. West Churchman concludes that it is virtually impossible to scientifically quantify measures of performance based on subjective ratings of library service by the user:

> Thus the scientist would find it extremely difficult at the present time to study the library of a university and try to construct a model of its effectiveness. He would not be able to tell whether the activities of the library are contributing to the measure of performance of the library system, i.e., to user benefits. So he would think it quite impossible to determine whether the allocations that are made to various programs and subprograms are proper. And lastly, it would not be possible to determine the real value of the library for the larger system in which the library is embedded.[3]

How can one judge objectively, whether the allocation of $10,000 or, for that matter $50,000, would be sufficient to purchase the materials to satisfy the needs of a fourth-year honors Physics student doing a major research paper?

In 'lean' times, when a collection budget is static or has been cut, collection budget allocation methods are rigorously scrutinized by all disciplines. A threshold in the collection funding of each discipline can be reached, below which allocation formula are no longer perceived as a 'fair and equitable' method of dividing funds, but as the root cause of the problem of inadequate funding for a discipline. The most sophisticated formula is useless if sufficient funds are unavailable to meet the minimum demands of a discipline.

During my research on formula and collection allocation models, I found that many factors were not considered. Outside funding agencies' decisions, economic and social factors affecting the number of students attending the university, and collection usage, were seldom considered important to the formula I examined in the literature. I came to the conclusion that, in Laurentian's situation, the majority of problems arose as a result of not having a mechanism to change and judge the merits of previous allocation decisions. A more all-encompassing approach had to be taken to the problem of finding a 'fair and equitable' method of dividing collection funds amongst the various disciplines that would incorporate more of the outside factors affecting collection funding.

A library collection development model incorporating this approach, and based on a realistic assessment of the library's objectives and economic resources, was developed to include outside factors that impacted library funding decisions. The library collection development model proposed consists of two parts as illustrated in Figures 1a and 1b. Figure 1a outlines the input and the decision factors that are considered in allocating current collection funds. Figure 1b contains the Supply and Demand Time Frame Chart created annually on the macro level (Figure 1c) for the entire collection budget and at the micro level (Figure 1d) for each discipline. Previous allocation decisions can be judged on their success or failure to meet the three basic types of library objectives on which the allocation decisions are made. The process of annual evaluation is incorporated into the collection development model, and is the mechanism whereby disciplines can judge the effectiveness of previous funding decisions.

There are three types of objectives or goals that are considered in this model: (1) User-oriented: the needs of the users as perceived by the user and the library staff who serve them; (2) Funder-oriented: the criteria, policies, constraints and decision processes involved in

FIGURE 1a. A Library Development Model to Allocate Resources to Meet User Demands

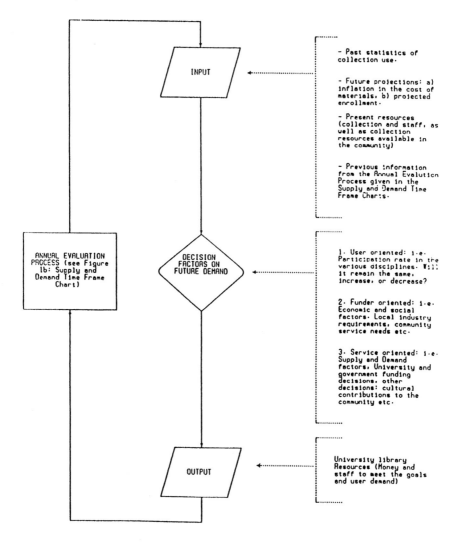

FIGURE 1b. The Supply and Demand Time Frame Chart

```
Goals &                                    ---SUPPLY    Objectives
                      ***DEMAND

    3 | ---           ---           ----          ---
      | ****          ***           **            ***


    2 | ----          ----          ---           ---
      | ****          ****          **            ***


    1 | -----         ----          --            ----
      | ***           **            ****          ***

TIME  | Immediate     Short Term    Intermediate  Long Term
FRAME |                                                      ----------------------
----->
```

funding the library; (3) Service-oriented: the needs of the library staff in providing the services. These goals or objectives can then be placed on a Supply and Demand Time Frame Chart and can be subdivided into immediate, short term, intermediate and long term, both on a macro level for the entire library and a micro level for each discipline requiring collection funding.

Budget Priorities Based on User Demand

One of the most important areas in the Annual Evaluation Process outlined in the model is assessing user demand. If an item is purchased and is never used within a reasonable time frame there has to be a mechanism, whereby selection and/or the allocation decisions can be questioned for each discipline. Collecting data for the Supply and Demand Time Frame Charts includes the maintenance of past circulation statistics, current acquisitions lists, and a yearly questionnaire on the immediate, intermediate and long term needs for each discipline. Once the data is collected, the decision factors on future demand have to be considered. The economic impact of factors outside the library are then considered in the decision process.

FIGURE 1c. Annual Distribution of the Collection Budget Between the Disciplines (MACRO Level Supply/Demand Chart)

	DEMAND			SUPPLY			
Discipline	Faculty Complement	Student Courses	Research Rated:1-5	Periodicals Purchased	Monographs Purchased	Current 1978-9 Dollar Allotment	Constant Dollar Allotment Allowing for a Decrease in Purchasing Power of 15% since 1973-4
Classics	1	21	1	5	16	250.00	212.50
English	12	701	3	131	325	10,000.00	8,500.00
Français	14	654	3	87	325	8,700.00	7,395.00
Modern Lang.	7	329	3	126	195	6,500.00	5,525.00
Philosophy	4	313	2	94	133	3,600.00	3,060.00
Economics	10	597	2	131	198	8,000.00	6,800.00
Geography	9	443	4	116	175	7,000.00	5,950.00
History	12	435	4	176	315	12,200.00	10,370.00
Political Sci.	11	549	3	111	219	8,000.00	6,800.00
Psychology	15	1032	4	145	313	12,000.00	10,200.00
Sociology	18	1110	4	137	277	10,000.00	8,500.00
Biology	9	517	5	160	113	19,350.00	16,447.50
Chemistry	10	411	5	87	103	21,500.00	18,275.00
Geology	8	185	5	127	92	13,400.00	11,390.00
Mathematics	6	377	3	74	118	10,050.00	8,542.50
Physics	9	361	5	117	127	19,700.00	16,745.00
Commerce	17	1268	2	94	241	9,500.00	8,075.00
Engineering	9	265	3	57	50	2,000.00	1,700.00
Nursing	11	218	2	65	108	4,500.00	3,825.00
Phy. Education	15	755	2	116	229	6,500.00	5,525.00
Social Work	8	586	2	60	138	4,400.00	3,740.00
Translators	9	496	1	20	94	2,000.00	1,700.00
Canadian Stud.	1	21	2	3	120	2,000.00	1,700.00
Child Devel.	1	120	2	10	60	1,000.00	850.00
Law & Justice	1	130	2	2	38	600.00	510.00
S.P.A.D.	1	141	1	2	60	1,000.00	850.00
TOTALS	235	3892	75	2253	4182	203,750.00	173,187.50

FIGURE 1d. Estimated and Actual Supply and Demand Chart for Each Discipline (MICRO Supply/Demand Diagram)

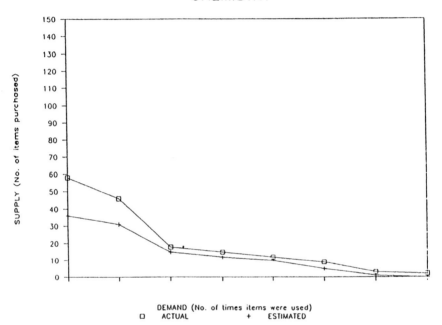

CHEMISTRY

DEMAND (No. of times items were used)
□   ACTUAL   +   ESTIMATED

The Economic Impact of Outside Funding Agencies

On what economic basis are funds being provided, by whom, and what criteria are funding agencies using to allocate resources to a library? A 1% drop in overall funding to a university could result in a 50% decrease in library collection funding. A 1% drop in government revenue could result in a 5% decrease in university funding, depending on the priorities of the government. It is of critical importance, therefore, to try and understand the process and the potential effects outside funding agencies' decisions can have on a library's budget.

Libraries must be seen in the context of:

a dynamic system constantly changing and adjusting in response to the demands being made on it by its socio-economic environment. Thus, we have the picture of a complex dynamic system composed of several major subsystems (acquisitions, cataloguing, circulation, and others) in constant evolution. In addition, the major subsystems are intimately interconnected, interdependent, and interacting constantly with each other.[4]

One of the difficulties of allocating limited collection funds stems from the fact that libraries are usually dependent on two or three levels of outside funding. In Laurentian's case, the library is dependent on the university for funding, who in turn is dependent on the provincial government, who in turn is dependent on transfer payment programs from the federal government, the general health of the economy, the demands of other governmental services and agencies, and ultimately, the public, for funding.

Patterns and Trends in Funding

The study of educational spending in the Province of Ontario provides an interesting insight into funding responses. It is D. K. Foot's contention that Ontario government expenditures over a twenty-five year period in the areas of highway, education, health and social services exhibit a co-ordinated development pattern.[5] A clear pattern emerges every 5 to 8 years in which a new area or function receives concentrated attention of the provincial government, resulting in a rapid growth in expenditures until some 'desired' level of expenditure is achieved, after which the growth rate is curtailed and the process begins again with some other area that needs attention. Foot concludes that it takes about two years on average to complete 50%, and four years to complete 75% of the desired adjustment.

Understanding the pattern and timing of outside funding agency spending can be extremely helpful in forecasting and planning a library budget over the medium and longer term (2-6 years). Caution must be used in placing too much faith on forecasting outside funding agency funding patterns. As Bertram M. Gross states:

estimates of presumed results must take into account many possible causative factors other than the program under analysis, and that many of such factors, being social, psychological, and political in nature, are not readily understandable in terms of economics or any other single discipline. Moreover in real life, benefits and disbenefits (no matter how calculated) are never disembodied. They are enjoyed or suffered by real people, groups, or institutions and some power wielders will always fail to welcome, or even be amused by, frank answers to the question of just whose ox has been gored or fed.[6]

The above statement is an important reminder that estimating techniques are just that and should not be substituted for good judgement in library planning decisions.

Inaccuracies of Enrollment Forecasting Models and Formula

The inaccuracies of forecasting future university enrollment during the seventies can be aptly demonstrated by the following figures:

	Projected	Actual	Difference
1976-77	217,900	164,989	(52,911) students or -24.2%
1977-78	234,700	159,293	(75,407) students or -32%

The above projections were made in 1970 and after seven years, were 32% off-target.[7] A 32% difference between the projected and actual figures is statistically significant and cannot be ignored. On what basis were these projections made? Was there any way of refining the forecasts to more accurately reflect actual enrollment?

The enrollment forecasts made in 1970 were based on two factors: (1) Participation rates in the general population in university attendance at that time, and (2) population age distribution statistics. Population age distribution statistics have in the past been, and continue to be, overemphasized as a factor in forecasting future enrollment trends in universities. This forecasting technique is appropriate for primary and secondary school enrollment projections, where attendance in such institutions is mandatory for all members of the 'school age' population; however, it is not an effective technique for university enrollment projections.

The participation rate of the general population is important, and is not based solely on graduates of secondary school age, but also on members of the adult population who wish to participate in continuing education programs. In 1970, the number of secondary school students going on to university was 32% and, therefore, it was assumed that the participation rate would remain the same or increase slightly as it had in the previous decade.

What was not foreseen at that time was that the participation rate in university education is a far more complex variable, composed of many other factors. The job market for graduates, the popularity of Community College Programs, the rising costs of a university education are all variable factors which affect the participation rate of prospective university students. Most enrollment forecasting models refuse to consider subjective factors, and as a result, will continue to have a statistically significant error rate.

How often has it been said that forecasting is merely a guessing game with no one held responsible for the accuracy of their forecasts? Unfortunately, the consequences of inaccurate forecasting can be enormous. Forecasts are used by government and university planners to initiate new buildings, hire personnel, declare redundancies, and to plan for program growth areas.

Viewing Enrollment Participation from a Different Economic Perspective

One of the principle economic laws of supply and demand can help us understand why enrollment projections based on current or past participation rates of the general population are so inaccurate. Reformulated based on the principle of supply and demand, one can conclude that as the number of university students diminishes because of a decreasing demand for their qualifications, a shortage in the market is eventually created which in turn creates a new demand for more graduates with those qualifications.

What significance should this principle have for budgeting decisions in university libraries? In planning for the future using an economic theory of library development, current funding would be provided to those disciplines where potential growth is expected. The decision to fund a discipline would not be based *solely* on current and past circulation, the current size of faculty or student complements, or other usage statistics. Traditional collection allocation formula have usually weighted current usage factors as prime indicators of future demand *increasing* budget allotments to those disciplines who are or have already expanded. In contrast, an economic development model based on the principle of supply and demand can be used to anticipate a decreasing demand from current growth disciplines, and can be used to adjust collection allocation decisions accordingly.

A basic problem with such a model lies in forecasting the future supply and demand equation for each discipline. Who decides which discipline will be expanded in the future? Hard data is not available to answer this dilemma, and usually it is left to a subjective consensus of university planners. Projecting future economic and social trends are considered by most economic forecasters as 'subjective' factors, and are given no weight in allocation formula, because such factors are seen as unscientific and are not based on 'hard' data. As a result, most formula and collection allocation models are based on a mirror of the present and the past, rather than a projection of future user needs.

Innovative efforts will be required to re-examine current collection allocation methods to incorporate supply and demand theory, as well as 'subjective' factors. This will not be a simple task as constant revision will be required of allocation formula and models to incorporate factors which are not easily measured. Some of the most important planning decisions have to be based on factors that cannot be measured, and only the results can be measured.

The collection allocation model proposed in Figure 1 does not attempt to weight the decision factors. The weighting process requires library planners and decision makers to take both subjective and objective factors into account before allocating collection funding. A feedback mechanism to identify projection errors of demand or use is built into the model. By identifying why and on what assumptions a previous decision was made to allocate resources, refinements can be made to future allocation decisions. The process of continuous change in the economic environment is assumed.

Simulation Model Used to Calculate
the Purchasing Power of the Collection Budget

It is useful for planning purposes to have a library purchasing power model or formula based on the present economic environment in order to simulate the impact of budget proposals before allocation decisions are made. Figures 2a, b, and c simulate a static, a decreasing, and an increasing total library budget situation. The following formula is used as a basis for the simulation models illustrated:

$$NI = \frac{TB + or - \%ITB - FC + or - \%IFC}{AC + or - \%IAC}$$

where NI is the total number of items that can be purchased. TB is the present total budget, ITB is the increase or decrease in the present total budget, FC is a variable representing fixed costs (staffing, maintenance, equipment, supplies, etc.), IFC is the increase or decrease in the present fixed costs, AC is the present average cost of the items, and IAC is the increase or decrease in the average cost of the items.

By using different % values in the above formula, useful simulations can be made on the impact of current budget proposals. The formula is based solely on the present ratio of fixed costs to collection funds. This simulation tool is only one of the forecasting methods that is proposed in the Library Development Model illustrated in Figure 1.

Service-Oriented Objectives and Goals

The Library Collection Development Model contains a third set of objectives or goals that are termed 'Service-oriented.' These are the economic, social, psychological, and other needs of the library staff providing the services. Salaries, working conditions, job satisfaction, leadership, organizational structure are only a few of the many needs of library staff. Books and periodicals cannot be purchased or catalogued, adequate statistics on collection use cannot be obtained, without a well-organized, trained, and motivated library staff.

FIGURE 2a. Forecast Model of a Static Total Library Budget

FISCAL YEAR	$1,000,000	$700,000	$300,000	$30.00	10,000	ASSUMPTIONS
Current	$1,000,000	$749,000	$251,000	$31.80	7,893	---- Total Budget (Remaining static)
1	$1,000,000	$801,430	$198,570	$33.71	5,890	---- Fixed costs (7% increase per year. This assumes salary cuts of 2% per year.)
2	$1,000,000	$857,530	$142,470	$35.73	3,987	---- Collection Purchasing Funds (In current dollars)
3	$1,000,000	$917,557	$82,443	$37.87	2,177	---- Average cost of purchasing library materials (6% increase annually)
4						---- Number of items purchased for the Collection

208

FIGURE 2b. Forecast Model of a Decreasing Total Library Budget

FISCAL YEAR	Current	1	2	3	4	ASSUMPTIONS
	$1,000,000	$980,000	$960,400	$941,192	$922,368	---- Total Budget (Decreasing by 2% per year)
	$700,000	$749,000	$801,430	$857,530	$917,557	---- Fixed costs (7% increase per year. This assumes salary cuts of 2% per year.)
	$300,000	$231,000	$158,970	$83,662	$4,811	---- Collection Purchasing Funds (In current dollars)
	$30.00	$31.80	$33.71	$35.73	$37.87	---- Average cost of purchasing library materials (6% increase annually)
	10,000	7,264	4,715	2,341	127	---- Number of items purchased for the Collection

FIGURE 2c. Forecast Model of an Increasing Total Library Budget

FISCAL YEAR	Current	1	2	3	4	ASSUMPTIONS
	$1,000,000	$1,050,000	$1,102,500	$1,157,625	$1,215,506	---- Total Budget (Increasing by 5% annually)
	$700,000	$749,000	$801,430	$857,530	$917,557	---- Fixed costs (7% increase per year. This assumes salary cuts of 2% per year.)
	$300,000	$301,000	$301,070	$300,095	$297,949	---- Collection Purchasing Funds (In current dollars)
	$30.00	$31.80	$33.71	$35.73	$37.87	---- Average cost of purchasing library materials (6% increase annually)
	10,000	9,465	8,931	8,399	7,868	---- Number of items purchased for the Collection

Technological Change and Its Impact
on the Library Collection Model Outlined

Automated library systems are available that can break down collection usage by title, discipline and category of user. Such systems are usually fully integrated: acquisitions, cataloguing, and circulation data are immediately available, making the task of measuring collection usage by discipline and calculating simulation models and formula much easier. Quantitative statistics can be easily maintained on a wide range of economic factors from collection usage to the average costs of materials for each discipline. What cannot be measured by automated systems is the qualitative side of budget forecasting, the subjective factors of user satisfaction with a collection, decisions on future growth areas, and other service factors.

Other service factors may include: reliance on inter-library loan for expensive journal subscriptions, and co-operative collection development projects between libraries, to assist in reducing the strain on static or reduced collection budgets. Telefacsimile transmission of documents will decrease the need for duplicating expensive journals, and will allow libraries to concentrate funding on other areas of the collection, or to improve access to other collections.

No university library collection is totally self-sufficient in all disciplines. Building a comprehensive collection in even a few areas may be impossible in 'lean' times. Access to information, rapid document delivery, co-operative efforts to rationalize collection purchases between institutions, can have more profound results in meeting immediate user demands than wasting a great deal of effort attempting to divide an inadequate collection budget amongst a variety of disciplines.

CONCLUSION

The Library Development Model proposed provides a more encyclopedic method of examining the many factors that contribute to 'fair and equitable' decisions on allocating collection funds. In the process of weighting all the factors, subjective and objective decisions have to be made, based on the collective judgement of many individuals. The decision process is made easier by using clearly stated objectives, goals, and assumptions which in turn can be used to judge the fairness of applying economic resources to meet user demand. The decision process recommended can be accepted, rejected, or modified as circumstances dictate, because the collection development model proposed contains a re-evaluation process as part of the Annual Evaluation Process. Advances in technology and other methods of increasing access to information will assist, but will never replace, the need for longer term collection budget allocation decisions.

REFERENCES

1. Council of Ontario Universities. An Uncertain Future: review 1975-76 to 1977-78. Toronto: COU, 1979.

2. The following is a selective list of references dealing with collection allocation methods and formula budgeting:

R. E. Burton. "Formula budgeting: an example," Special Libraries, 66 (February 1975): 61-67.

B. H. Dillehay. "Book budget allocation: subjective or objective approach," Special Libraries, 62 (December 1971): 509-14.

S. D. Gold. "Allocating the book budget: an economic model," College & Research Libraries, 36 (September 1975): 397-402.

S. K. Goyal. "Allocation of library funds to different departments of a university: an operational research approach," College & Research Libraries, 34 (May 1973): 219-22.

Francis Landon Greaves. "The allocation formula as a form of Book fund management in selected State-Supported Academic Libraries." Ph.D. dissertation, Florida State University, 1974.

J. J. Kohut. "Allocating the book budget: a model," College & Research Libraries, 35 (May 1974): 192-9.

J. J. Kohut and J. F. Walker. "Allocating the Book Budget: Equity and Economic Efficiency," College & Research Libraries, 36 (September 1975): 403-410.

W. E. McGrath. "Pragmatic book allocation formula for academic and public libraries with a test for its effectiveness," Library Resources and Technical Services, 19 (Fall 1975): 356-69:

Thomas John Pierce. "The Economics of Library Acquisitions: A Book Allocation Model for University Libraries." Ph.D. dissertation, University of Notre Dame, 1976.

D. Revill. "Bookfund allocation formula," New Library World, 75 (August 1974): 162-3.

G. S. Sampson. "Allocating the book budget: Measuring for inflation," College & Research Libraries, 39 (September 1978): 381-3.

R. J. Welwood. "Book budget allocations: an objective formula for the small academic library," Canadian Library Journal, 34 (June 1977): 213-220.

3. Churchman, C. West. The Systems Approach. New York: Dell Publishing Co., 1968, p. 107.

4. David L. Raphael. The Systems concept and the Library in Administration and Change: Continuing education in Library Administration. Rutgers: Rutgers University Press, 1969, p. 56.

5. D. K. Foot. Provincial Public Finance in Ontario: an empirical analysis of the last twenty-five years. Toronto: Ontario Economic Council, 1977, p. 174-5.

6. Bertram M. Gross, "The New Systems Budgeting," Public Administration Review, 29 (March-April 1969), p. 133.

7. The statistics were taken from two sources. The projected figures can be found in Z. E. Zsigmond's Enrollment in Educational Institutions by Province 1951-51 to 1980-81. Ottawa: Queen's Printer, 1970, p. 127.

The actual figures can be found in the Ontario Council on University Affairs Fifth Annual Report, 1978-79. Toronto: Queen's Printer, 1979, p. 50.

SPECIAL REPORTS

Choice at a Distance:
A Footnote for an Official History

Robert S. Bravard

SUMMARY. This personal essay is a recollection of the author's experiences as a consultant during the early years of the review magazine, *Choice*. Included are personal glimpses of the first two editors and an indication of their personalities. The dismissal of the second *Choice* editor is described from the point of view of a sympathetic outsider.

I can't remember now where I first read the announcement of the plans to start an academic library oriented review magazine to be called *Choice*. My wife thinks she saw the notice first in *Library Journal*; I have a vague memory of reading it somewhere in the *New York Times*. It certainly doesn't matter now; I wrote immediately for an application and as a result became one of their twenty-five year "consultants."

The first book I reviewed was also a first and, as it has turned out, the only collection of poems by one Alvin Feinman. I can recall this first review vividly for two reasons. The book arrived just

Robert S. Bravard is Director of Library Services, Stevenson Library, Lock Haven University, Lock Haven, PA 17745.

215

before the death of my father and it took all the discipline he had instilled in me to focus on reviewing anything. And, as every "consultant" on record has mentioned, I remember the difficulty of concentrating my thoughts into the space limitation. The arrival of a copy of the second issue of *Choice* with its soon familiar dull orange cover and the first to have a review by me was a pleasant moment. Over the years, the issues piled up; they made a formidable appearance in one corner of my office at home.

My relationship with Choice from the beginning was a comfortable one. Back in those early days, the founding editor himself, Richard Gardner, sometimes answered the telephone. Dr. Gardner, as he is now, seemed fascinated by what the magazine was trying to do and I enjoyed our conversations covering a wide range of shared interests across the literary board.

The early Sixties were truly exciting times, especially for serious readers. Almost every month, or so it seemed, another of the legendary improper books that were not in any American small college library was being published by Grove Press. Authors, such as Jean Genet and Henry Miller who had only been hinted about in comparative lit classes, were suddenly absolutely available in paperback. In addition to the hardback edition, there were at least three paperback editions of *Lady Chatterly's Lover*. In one of my phone conversations with Dr. Gardner I mentioned the kick of being a librarian at this moment and how only professional timidity was holding back the availability of these notorious books for serious readers.

Dr. Gardner insisted that I write about this. Thanks to his encouragement and his persistence, the May, 1965, issue of *Choice* carried my first effort at professional writing. My stock soared at my home campus; the then Director of Library Services even extracted the article, put it in a pamphlet binder and cataloged it. I have to admit that when I in turn became the Library Director one of my earliest acts was to remove this from the collection.

Dr. Gardner also caused me to experience a most unexpected telephone call. One day I received a call from the Academic Dean of Parsons College out in Iowa. Parsons in those days was possibly the most notorious college in the country; as long as one paid one's tuition, one remained enrolled. I was being offered right then and there over the phone the job of Acquisitions Librarian. A rather high materials budget was indicated. Startled at this, I asked how I had become of interest to them. The Dean informed me that I had been the sole person recommended by Dick Gardner and that I had been characterized as one of the best "book men" in the country. The job was absolutely mine as soon as I said yes. Instead, I asked for a copy of the catalog and promised to make up my mind as soon as I had looked it over. The catalog arrived; there was almost no one listed with more than two years employment at Parsons. I stayed at Lock Haven. Still I was quite flattered by Dr. Gardner's characterization of me, and when I thanked him he gently said he was only speaking the truth. It was heady stuff.

In 1966, Richard Gardner moved on. After a search, a new editor was named: Peter Doiron. At that moment, so far as I was concerned, little change seemed to take place. My review copies arrived regularly, the reviews were printed, and another copy of the magazine joined the stack. The transition, from the perspective of a consultant, was without incident. There was not a hint that five years later *Choice* would experience perhaps the single most traumatic event in its history.

My first official communication from Mr. Doiron was a letter of censure. Had events been as they must have appeared to him, the letter would have been deserved. Happily, events were not as they appeared.

I had gone to a Pennsylvania Library Association meeting held in the state capitol of Harrisburg. Since I was in those days the Head Technical Services Librarian with a considerable responsibility for collection development, I headed straight for the exhibitors' area. Soon I came across the table of Folklore Associates of Hatboro, Pennsylvania. They were essentially a reprint house but did have a handful of doctoral dissertations centered on urban folklore. I recognized some of the titles; thought it was a worthy project; took a list; promised an order; and struck up a conversation with as it turned out the owner. Since it was that time of day, he invited me to lunch.

Over the meal, which he made clear he was paying for, we talked about this and that. Then he asked me how he could get his new titles reviewed so librarians would notice them. I instantly mentioned *Choice* and told him where it was. I also told him that I didn't review books in this area. He took down the information and we finished lunch. As soon as I was back in the Library, we placed an order for a substantial number of the books (remember the days when libraries had money?) and the lunch quickly faded from memory.

Apparently after returning home, the publisher wrote the editor of *Choice* a most forceful letter; apparently, I was mentioned by name and it was strongly suggested that the books be sent to me for review. On the surface I had violated most of the canons of my consultancy. Peter Doiron wrote a stinging letter.

After gathering my thoughts, I knew that I was innocent and began to draft a letter. It was late afternoon and the letter just didn't seem to want to come together. Finally I picked up the phone and got Peter Doiron.

When he came on the line I told the editor who I was. He remembered me all right. I quickly and calmly told him that there had been a misunderstanding and briefly indicated what had happened. By the end of the conversation we were on a Bob and Peter basis. Peter told me to forget about the letter; he would pull it from my file. I wonder if he remembered to do so. Anyhow, I was now on a telephone basis with the second *Choice* editor.

This would be about 1967. Again, something very interesting was taking place in the publishing world. Grove Press had managed to publish just about every significant banned work; once you have published the Marquis de Sade, who is left? In 1966, Stephen Marcus had broken off his major study of the work of Charles Dickens to publish *The Other Victorians, A Study of Sexuality and Pornography in Mid-Nineteenth-Century England* (N.Y., Basic Books, 1966). In this landmark work, Marcus demonstrated what could be learned from the erotic writing of a given period. In the wake of the Grove Press breakthrough and a series of Supreme Court decisions freeing up the publishing of just about any print work, Grove Press and a host of paperback presses were printing the entire corpus of Victorian and Edwardian pornography. For a while there it seemed as though everything included in Henry Spence Ashbee's three volume *Bibliobraphy of Forbidden Books* had become available at once.

All of this was politely ignored by the official library press. It seemed to me then and still makes sense to me that it was inappropriate for the custodians of the bibliographic record to ignore in toto one of the major publishing enterprises of this or any time. I tried to express these thoughts in a letter that appeared in the November 1, 1967 issue of *Library Journal*. In the letter, I suggested that the very least librarians could do was to record a list of what was published.

Shortly thereafter while I was talking to Peter he referred to my *LJ* letter. We talked a bit about what I had written; finally he said in effect why don't you do it for *Choice*. He promised to run the piece as an "In the Balance" article. I indicated a lack of funds or frequent opportunity to gather materials; Peter told me he would take care of that. Apparently a few of the paperback erotic publishers were shipping review copies up to *Choice*; not long after a very large box arrived and I was all at once a dirty book bibliographer.

At this point, I should indicate two points of autobiography. First, all my life I have been a First Amendment absolutist; I believed and continue to believe that there is no valid reason for censoring anything. If good ideas and writing cannot win over bad ideas and writing, then the good does not deserve to win. Second, I had, shall we say, abandoned my head librarianship previous to arriving at Lock Haven State College over the issue of censorship. It also helped that I have the gift to read at a rate far higher than average.

The article itself was rather easy to write; it still, at least to me, seems to hold up fairly well. The bibliography was another matter. I methodically worked my way through that large box, skimming the books, recording the bibliographic data, and giving a hint of the contents. I will admit that the first one I read was stimulating; however, the second one was much less so. After that it was something like reading a plumber's manual.

There was one bonus. The occasional well written book came as a welcome surprise. My favorite was and remains *Teleny*, a late Victorian item; according to a very persistent legend, the committee of fin de siecle writers who created *Teleny* included Oscar Wilde. Based on the text alone, I am inclined to think there may be some truth to this. For the first time I read the short story, "Only a Boy," which is universally attributed by journalists to none other than the author of *Poems of Childhood*, Eugene Field. The notorious closet drama of the Earl of Rochester, *Sodom*, was indeed indecent. I was startled to come across the *Memoirs of Josephine Mutzenbacher*, which in some Germanic quarters is attributed to none other than Felix Salten. Perhaps he wrote it as an anecdote to all that Bambi stuff.

Throughout the drafting and revision of the piece, Peter Doiron was encouraging, helpful, and genuinely supportive. His was a model of editorial guidance. Our only mild disagreement was over my annotation to the only gay entry in the bibliography, *The Loon Songs Trilogy* by Richard Amory; he compromised with me describing the work as "a contemporary homosexual idyll" and Peter writing the rest of the annotation. In addition, Peter followed my piece with a brief essay and bibliography of his own, " Responsibility." I thought, all in all, that we had in the spirit of the times done something commendable.

If I had it to do over, I would have used a different title; both Peter and I missed that one. At the time I was writing the article, Grove Press in its advertisements and in the *Evergreen Review* (Does anybody remember that controversial literary journal?) was making the case for "black" literature. Grove Press even had called its series of hard cover printings of Edwardian erotica the "Black Circle" series. So I typed out a title, "A Librarian's Guide to Black Literature." I wonder now over the years how many librarians I managed to trick into reading about erotica. Sometimes one can be too focused on the subject at hand for one's own good.

The essay-bibliography ran in the October, 1968 issue of *Choice*. At first there seemed to be no reaction from anybody. After a couple of months I mentioned my surprise at this lack of reaction to Peter. After some hesitation, he finally indicated to me that perhaps such was not the case. "Oh," I said, "What do you mean?"

Peter then said that he had received some very strong reaction from headquarters, the American Library Association offices in Chicago. It was my first hint from anybody that there was a level of tension between the American Library Association and *Choice*. Peter did not go into details, but he did suggest that some of it was personal. He also said that the article really shocked a lot of important people at A.L.A. I persisted in asking who; I could not imagine in 1968 that this solemn piece would bother anybody.

Peter told me he had received a cool telephone call from Judith Krug; according to him, Ms. Krug stated that this was not the sort of exercise in academic freedom that *Choice* should be engaging in. I could hardly believe that the chief dragoon of the Office of Intellectual Freedom would hint at censorship, but Peter insisted that such was the case. Then Peter dropped his bombshell; he had written to the editor of the *Newsletter on Intellectual Freedom*, LeRoy Charles Merritt, to direct his attention to the *Choice* articles. Mr. Merritt read the articles and was quite offended. A second phone call from Peter was a warning that Mr. Merritt was going to scold us in public in the next issue of the *Newsletter*.

Well, LeRoy Charles Merritt did have an "Editorial Epistle" on page 12 of the January, 1969, *Newsletter on Intellectual Freedom*. It did not seem to me to be much of a scolding; I found it more a confused and confusing personal reaction. When I told Peter this, he mildly remarked that "they" had insisted that Mr. Merritt tone his piece down. I thought about writing a reply but in the press of events let it pass. I did think the entire episode a bit unusual.

Not long after the appearance of the "Editorial Epistle," Peter called and asked if I was up to a second article. He, with amusement, told me that an enterprising West Coast dealer in erotic paperbacks had gathered together every title on the *Choice* list and was selling it as a unit; the dealer had also reprinted my essay, with Peter's permission. Peter also told me that additional publishers were now eager to send review copies of their offerings. I indicated that I thought I could do another list and the shipments began again.

This time Peter did not seem bothered at the possibility of my including gay material. We agreed that this list would be representational of what was available out there. I set to work and eventually the November, 1970, issue of *Choice* ran "American Erotica at the Close of the Sixties." Rereading it now, I find it to be a pretty good photograph of the way things were at a specific time. The only phrase I truly would wish to take back is a much too flippant reference to child abuse.

Throughout this period, I was handling my regular review responsibilities. A steady stream of materials came along and was duly read and reviewed. Even though I was personally close to the editor, I never had the notion that as a consultant I was ever given any special treatment. The editing clearly went on and an occasional review was sent back for clarification.

When Peter called me a couple of months after the article ran, he did not mention any unfavorable reactions from A.L.A. Headquarters or anybody else. As a matter of fact, the only reaction I ever received directly was a sad letter from an individual out in North Dakota asking for the address of the newspaper of the erotic film industry, *The Exploiter*; I sent it.

At the end of the second *Choice* article, I engaged in a little offhand social predicting. I proclaimed a "resounding change in the American moral climate"; I know better now. And with Peter's encouragement, I indicated "our intention to attempt to make this bibliography an annual or biannual occurrence." Peter had even asked me if I could find someone in the visual arts field to review pictorial works and I had succeeded in doing so. By now my bibliographic listing/annotating were routine. The third bibliography was developing in draft form. Both Peter and I had decided to limit the introductory material to a few paragraphs.

There were now frequent indications from Peter that he was hearing much more than he cared to from A.L.A. Headquarters. Peter seemed most at odds with the then Executive Director of A.L.A., David Clift; often the irritations seemed to be quite personal, almost a matter of individual personal styles in conflict. Every once in a while I would gently ask Peter if he really had to go out of his way to annoy David Clift; Peter would insist that Clift was a master of petty retaliations. I also recall the disquieting news items in the library press concerning problems with managerial matters. I can truthfully say that to me Peter seemed cheerful, eager to continue the bibliography, and, in telephone conversations, at ease. Later, much later, there were those who indicated to me that such was not always the case.

Obviously I was living far away from whatever was going on between Peter Doiron and David Clift. I still have copies of my letters to Peter in June and July, all totally focused on developing the third bibliography. The now yellowing copy of the letter of July 2 thanked Peter for his phone call and in passing noted that his "news was really encouraging." If my memory serves, the news was about A.L.A., but I have no way of confirming that now. My next letter was written on July 13.

During the first week in August it crossed my mind that I still hadn't had a reply from Peter so I called. There was nothing unusual about this; if *Choice* business was pressing, he might well be too busy to write me about a developing article. The phone was answered and I announced, as I had many times, "This is Bob Bravard at Lock Haven, is Peter in?" There was a long, long silence and then the secretary whispered, "Oh, Mr. Bravard, don't you know what's gone on here?" Clearly I did not know. She took my number and told me she would call me back within a few minutes.

Her return call, judging from the background noise, was from a public telephone. What I learned for the first time and what the library world was to be told officially by A.L.A. about the event could be summarized in the first sentence of the report in the September 15, 1971, issue of *Library Journal*: "In a meeting held in a Hartford, Connecticut hotel room on July 29, 1971, Peter M. Doiron was summarily dismissed as editor of *Choice* . . . " The secretary told how Peter was summoned to a meeting at Hartford and apparently as soon as he was in the hotel a phone call was made to Middletown. A crew of large men abruptly entered the *Choice* offices and without any notice of any sort began changing the office locks. The men were, in her words, rude, threatening, and abusive of the entire office staff. Peter was not allowed to return to the office to pick up his personal belongings during regular office hours; only after hours was he escorted in and watched as he collected his things. Someone stood by and made a list of everything he took. By the time the secretary had described these events, she was sobbing — deep terrible sobs. It is not a moment I enjoy remembering.

There was, of course, a considerable uproar across the American library world. Peter himself tried to fight back. There was a petition effort led by E. J. Josey. I wrote a letter to the editor of *Library Journal*. In the end, nothing changed. David Clift and his A.L.A. allies artfully rode out the protests; Peter Doiron never had a chance. Clift drove A.L.A. over Peter Doiron like a steamroller going over a flower garden. It was coldly brutal and it was savagely effective. Few librarians were prepared for this level of hardball; it all sounded like an episode on one of those business novels so popular in the Fifties.

Why was Peter fired in such a vicious fashion? To this day no one outside A.L.A. headquarters knows for sure. There was vague talk of administrative problems, of inappropriate personal actions, and a lack of appropriate communications. Among these vague reasons there does not seem to be anything that could not have been resolved by a good consultant. There was also plenty of rumor and you could take your pick of alleged sexual misconducts. The A.L.A. "establishment" used innuendo masterfully. Here is a classic example of character assassination by indirect statement as contained in a letter dated October 20, 1971, from the then President of ACRL, Joseph H. Reason, to E. J. Josey: "We [the ACRL Board] reached this decision after giving full consideration to the facts which were available to us at that time because it was our considered opinion that disclosure of these facts would prove detrimental to Doiron's future. Facts which have become available since that meeting indicate that we made the proper decision. At one point I felt that a reporting to membership could be done if Doiron gave permission. At this time I feel strongly that such a report should not be made even though Doiron approved."

David Clift achieved an absolute victory. The next time I heard directly from Peter had to be around 1974 or '75. He had signed on to edit a review magazine for a Western publisher long associated with the library world. He asked me to be one of his reviewers and I instantly agreed. Shortly, I received a couple of novels in bound proofs, read them, wrote, and mailed the reviews. When I called Peter to ask if the reviews were all right, he didn't want to talk about that at all. He was very upset with certain, according to Peter, unmet but agreed-to conditions of employment and felt that the entire episode was a mistake on his part. It was no surprise when the reviews never appeared anywhere. I have not spoken with Peter since, and as far as I personally know, Peter Doiron has disappeared without a trace. The field of librarianship is hardly so overpopulated with creative talented individuals that it can afford to have discarded one so arbitrarily. I continue to believe that David Clift set out to destroy Peter Doiron as a librarian for personal reasons; he succeeded completely.

Choice happily was strong enough to survive the uproar. By 1972, Richard Gardner was back as the editor and the magazine was solidly and peacefully on course. I have no idea what went on behind the scenes. There have been a series of very able editors since but I have not had any direct contact with any of them. Over the years *Choice* has been blessed with as excellent a corps of assistant editors as any publication has ever experienced; they are uniformly helpful and considerate and my relationships with my editors has always been most cordial. The magazine has spun off the invaluable *Books for College Libraries*, one of the most valuable collection development tools around; I am proud to have had a hand in this. *Choice* is a good enterprise with which to be associated.

And what happened to the books that comprised the controversial *Choice* bibliographies? They are intact, along with the manuscripts of the essays, and even the notes for the never-to-be third bibliography. One day I packed the whole collection up and arranged to have it deposited at a nearby major research university library. Every once in a while I visit the "Robert S. Bravard Collection of Esoterica." I am told it has been used by graduate students.

I happen to think *Choice* was very fortunate in its first (and third) and second editors. Richard Gardner founded a first rate review magazine, set the course, and eventually steadied that course. He gathered a wide ranging, far reaching, and highly dedicated collection of consultants.

Peter Doiron was creative, expansive, and highly imaginative. It would have been fun to see where he might have taken *Choice*. As the twenty-fifth anniversary passes, it would seem appropriate to recall Peter at his best, challenging, daring, inspiring; this legacy is a rich one for anybody to have left. I don't know what justice for Peter Doiron would be, or even if it is yet possible, but I wish it could be achieved. So far as I know, at my distance, it is the only skeleton in the *Choice* closet and I think some resolution is long overdue.

Resource Sharing
in African Libraries:
Problems and Recommendations

A. A. Alemna

SUMMARY. This paper is an attempt at reviewing the issue of resource sharing in Africa. It provides a general overview of the principle of resource sharing and identifies various obstacles to its application such as political, cultural, social, economic and legal problems. Possible solutions to these problems are suggested which include the need for African librarians to appreciate the importance of resource sharing and the establishment of a task force to initiate and develop a system for sharing information and resources in the region. African librarians should also take advantage of regional organisations such as the Organisation of African Unity (O.A.U.) and Economic Community of West African States (ECOWAS) to provide the legal and governmental support for resource sharing. The writer concludes that despite the seemingly numerous problems, resource sharing has a future in Africa.

The idea of co-operation—working together towards the same end—is very alive among independent African countries. There are a number of attempts at political and economic cooperation such as the Organisation of African Unity (O.A.U.), the East African Community (E.A.C.), the Economic Community of West African States (ECOWAS) and other organisations in Northern and Southern Africa. So the idea of regional cooperation is very much part of our history.

It is in the area of information and bibliographic activity that the experience has not been so successful in Africa. Resource sharing

---

A. A. Alemna is Senior Lecturer, Department of Library and Archival Studies, University of Ghana, P.O. Box 60, Legon, Ghana.

227

among libraries in the region has not taken cognisance of the programmes and activities of regional and international organisations. Even in the development of sectoral information systems there has been very little cooperation among libraries in Africa. Despite the fact that no single library is able to purchase all the publications produced internationally, and that the achievement of such a goal is not even possible at the national level, it appears that the arguments in favour of resource sharing have not been heard by librarians in Africa.

The situation in Africa is rather so serious and unfortunate as there is evidence of progress in resource sharing among libraries in other developing countries especially those in the Caribbean.' These countries have taken advantage of the emergence of information systems either manual or computerised, to improve upon their resources. the participatory (or cooperative) mobilisation and use of resources has become even more necessary now in the face of rising costs and shrinking budgets in African libraries. Resource sharing will go a long way to extend the range of resources and services in African libraries.

PROBLEMS OF RESOURCE SHARING

The fact that there is no regional system of resource sharing among African libraries indicate either that there is no need for such a system, or that there are barriers preventing its establishment. It is the view of the writer that the latter is the case. An attempt is made to discuss these problems in the light of prevailing circumstances in Africa.

One of the major barriers to resource sharing in Africa is the political problem. It is common for people (especially in the Western World) to treat Africa as if it were a single unit. But this is hardly the case. There are several countries with different political systems in Africa. These countries have come under different colonial masters such as the English, French, Portuguese, etc. The existence of so many nation states makes resource sharing difficult because of the bureaucracy, national pride and feelings of independence which naturally exist in some situations, and the complexities of relationships between governing countries in Europe who still exercise authority in the region. Writing on Interlending in the Caribbean, Cornish[2] ascribes this as one of the major barriers in the Caribbean region. This applies to Africa as well.

There is also the linguistic barrier. This is a product of the political problem. Having come under the government of different countries, African countries tend to communicate better in the languages of the mother countries. A number of African countries cannot therefore easily communicate with each other. When it comes to the technicalities of resource sharing, this can cause major problems and misunderstandings.

Another product of the different political systems is the different legal systems which the various countries have inherited and developed. This can be a barrier to resource sharing as what is allowed in one country may be illegal in another, and therefore to supply copies of documents can contravene not only copyright laws but sometimes trade and tariff agreements too.

A precondition, essential for the successful implementation of resource sharing programmes, is adequate financial support. The corrugated and unreliable nature of the funding of library and information services in West Africa has been documented by Boadi and Harvard-Williams.[3] This unhealthy state of affairs is characteristic of all African countries and has been a crucial factor in the slow development of library services.

Related to the problem of funding is the existence of a wide variety of currencies in Africa. Apart from French-speaking countries of West Africa which have adopted the use of a similar currency tied to the French franc, all other countries have different currencies. This prevents the easy arrangements of payments for services and frustrates moves for resource sharing.

The condition of poverty means that materials are inadequate in African libraries. Considering the problem of inadequate library collections, it would seem that any attempt to promote the sharing of resources would be futile, since libraries not able to meet their own needs would not be able to meet the needs of others. Parker has stated that "Librarians cannot share what they do not have, and may feel that if too little is shared between too many, every one will end up with even less than they had to begin with."[4] This feeling is common in African libraries.

A comprehensive location tool for the individual countries in Africa is an essential prerequisite to resource sharing. There are at the moment about 20 countries (mostly in English-speaking countries) in Africa that have national bibliographies.[5] This situation appears at first glance not to be so unfavourable. A greater part of these aids, however, is almost unusable for the purpose of literacy acquisition along traditional lines. In some countries there exists no obligation to deposit a copy of each publication, sometimes this obligation excludes important printers such as the government printing office; frequently publishers fail to deliver titles despite the mandatory obligation. In the national bibliographies or in current literary registers, local publications are given lesser priority in terms of space than European and American publications. Titles are often incomplete and such details as place where published, publisher and date published are often lacking altogether.

Writing on the use of African national bibliographies as selection resources, Gorman[6] states that unpublished documents and non-book materials tend not to be listed in these bibliographies. Although theses, dissertations, manuscripts, reports and other unpublished documents on a wide range of subjects are rapidly increasing in quantity, they are subject to little or no bibliographic control in most African countries. Various films, phonograph recordings, tapes and photographs are produced in Africa but these are not included in the national bibliographies. Under these circumstances, therefore, the African bibliographies are often of limited use for resource sharing purposes.

There is little use in having a comprehensive system if it takes so long to supply items to one another. Communication is thus a major barrier to resource sharing in Africa. This applies to methods of requesting and supplying documents. In Africa, making requests for documents is as difficult as transmitting the document itself. Some countries in Africa are so tied up with their former colonial masters that it is often easier and faster for a country like Ghana to obtain a material from Britain than from its closest neighbour, Togo. Similarly, libraries in Togo obtain materials easier and faster from France than from Ghana. One reason for this is the poor postal and telecommunications network within the continent. Photocopies of journal articles from various libraries and transmitted by air mail or, better still, telefacsimile, may also take long periods of time since the necessary equipment is lacking in many libraries.

The absence of unified cataloguing rules, classification schemes, standard name and subject authority lists has a negative effect on resource sharing in Africa. This problem has also been cited by Ashoor[7] as a major barrier to cooperation and exchange of bibliographic information in the libraries of the Arabian Gulf Region. In the Western world, adherence to standardised procedures for bibliographic control of library materials has very much facilitated resource sharing activities. For example, the adoption and uniform application of Anglo-American Cataloguing Rules (AACR), Classification schemes like L.C. and Dewey, name and subject authority lists of the Library of Congress has been very helpful in sharing bibliographic information. Although these tools are used by many libraries in Africa, they have been expanded and modified to suit individual local needs. Because of differences in forms of names and emphasis on subject content, special name authority lists and subject heading guides have been devised in African libraries. This has created inconsistencies from country to country, thereby making resource sharing difficult.

Resource sharing can be quite a demanding venture in terms of staff strength and capabilities. There is thus the need for an adequate number of qualified librarians who are committed and ready to render service beyond their local confine. Inadequate staffing, especially at the professional level, has been identified as a major problem facing libraries in Africa.[8] This, no doubt, has affected library services in general, and resource sharing in particular, in the continent.

There are a number of psychological barriers which have to be identified if resource sharing is to succeed in Africa. In some cases, attempts at initiating cooperative ventures are regarded with suspicion because the individuals concerned regard each other as potential rivals. Persons with the same qualifications who are working in the same field of interest regard each single accomplishment by someone else as a threat to their own position in this imaginary but fierce struggle for survival.[9]

The organisational framework within which resource sharing projects would operate successfully do not also exist in some African countries. As Bowden puts it "the librarianship of developing countries is scattered with tombstones as memorials to the cooperative projects that died or of the corpses that barely cling to life."[10] This is a pathetic yet accurate account of the cooperative movement in librarianship in developing countries. This situation has arisen mainly because of the fact that most of the cooperative projects have been started without sufficient regard to the essential elements that would enhance their viability.

RECOMMENDATIONS

Having identified some of the barriers to resource sharing among African libraries, it is necessary to make various recommendations that will help to make the system viable. As a first step, African librarians must see the need to share resources. This also includes the willingness to eliminate all psychological barriers involved in cooperation. The lack of sufficient appreciation of these elements has significantly contributed to the failure of many cooperative ventures.

Secondly, a task force should be formed for the purpose of initiating and developing a system for sharing information and resources in the region. This task force should include representatives of large academic libraries, particularly those who have experience and are exposed to automated library systems. The task force should work concurrently on various fronts — legal, administrative, technical, bibliographic, etc. — to initiate work for a library network.

African libraries should use the presence of organisations such as the Organisation of African Unity (O.A.U.) and the Economic Community of West African States (ECOWAS) to provide the legal base and governmental support for the regional programmes. The acceptance of these responsibilities by the national governments would confirm their recognition of the importance of information and also their role in its development and use.

There is a need for an agreement of or standards for bibliographic procedure among libraries in Africa for achieving a reasonable level of cooperation and resource sharing. This could be achieved through the adoption of such regulatory devices as the ISBN's,

ISSN's and AACR2. While their adoption would achieve the immediate benefit of uniformity in bibliographic description, their inbuilt quality for use in both manual and automated systems would ensure the ultimate orderly transformation from the manual to the automated mode of operation.

There is also the need to develop appropriate systems and networks to facilitate sharing of resources. The investment in library networking will help in various ways such as reducing the cost of acquiring library materials and eliminating duplication in creating bibliographic records. Fortunately, over the last few years a number of libraries (mostly university and research libraries) in Africa have introduced automated library systems. It is hoped that the remaining libraries will follow suit soon.

There is no point in a number of libraries or countries cooperating if none of them is offering anything that the others want or need. Librarians in Africa must therefore attempt to build up comprehensive collections especially in the areas of science, technology and agriculture as these areas appear to be in more demand by libraries in Africa. Any system created should ensure that an adequate collection of such materials is available within that system.

The problem of funding can be solved if governments in Africa accept the fact that adequate and timely information provided by libraries can contribute to socioeconomic development. Libraries in the region should also develop simplified systems which will cut down costs. An agreed accounting system could be developed among the libraries and a generally accepted code of practice and procedure adopted to minimise costs. The recent moves by a number of African countries to adopt single currencies will go a long way to simplify matters.

There is little that libraries as such can do to improve communications in Africa. However they should press for improvements in their access to telex, telefacsimile and other new technological developments to ensure that they can exploit what is available in full. In the West African sub-region, the courier service has been tried with some degree of success in Nigeria and Ghana. The encouragement and widespread use of this supplementary service would help in improving interlibrary communication.

In order to solve the staffing problem, a number of countries in

Africa are establishing library schools. The problem of shortage of manpower however still persists and that would suggest that better manpower planning based on a much closer study of national and regional needs and a tailoring of the educational programmes to meet those requirements, would be needed.

CONCLUSION

It would appear from the problems listed above that a programme of resource sharing is not likely to succeed in Africa. But this is not the case. In many African countries, attempts are being made to put the infrastructure for resource sharing in place. What is required now is a concerted effort, largely at the national, but also to some extent at the international level, to remove some of the obstacles already discussed. There exist great opportunities for resource sharing in Africa, but this can only be achieved after considerable investment in equipment and training has been realised and some practical steps taken. To be effective and meaningful, any plan for resource sharing in Africa must enhance the entire area and include all the language groups — French, Portuguese and English-speaking countries.

REFERENCES

1. Henry, M. "Cooperation and Coordination in the English-speaking Caribbean: 1950-1987." *International Library Review*. Vol.21, No.1. January, 1989. pp. 47-57.

2. Cornish, G.P. "Interlending in the Caribbean: Questions, Problems and possible solutions" *Interlending and Document Supply*. Vol.17, No.2, 1989. pp. 35-41.

3. Boadi, B.Y. and P. Harvard-Williams. "The Funding of Library and Information Services in West Africa." *International Library Review*. Vol.16, No.1. January, 1984. pp. 21-24.

4. Parker, J. "Resource sharing in developing countries: objectives and obstacles." In *Resource Sharing in Developing Countries*. Munchen: Saur, 1979. p. 16.

5. Wolcke-Renk, I. "Acquisition of African literature — problems and challenges for bookdealer and librarian." *IFLA Journal*. Vol.10, No.4. 1984. p. 378.

6. Gorman, G.E. "African national bibliographies as selection resources." *International Library Review*. Vol.21, No.4. October, 1989. p. 505.

7. Ashoor, M.S. "Bibliographic networking in the Arabian Gulf Region: prospects and problems." *Resource sharing and Information networks*. Vol.4, No.2. 1989 p. 20.

8. Alemna, A.A. "Acquisitions and Collection development education in Ghana." *Library Acquisitions: Practice and Theory*. Vol.14, No.1. 1990. pp. 53-59.

9. Mchornbu, K. "On librarianship of poverty." *Libri* Vol.32, No.3. 1982. pp. 241-250.

10. Bowden, R. "The opportunities for, and problems of, regional cooperation in library services in developing countries." In *Resource Sharing in Developing Countries*. Munchen: Saur, 1979. p. 93.